Reason To Write

Strategies for Success in Academic Writing

INTERMEDIATE

Robert F. Cohen
and
Judy L. Miller

OXFORD

UNIVERSITY PRESS

OXFORD
UNIVERSITY PRESS

198 Madison Avenue
New York, NY 10016 USA
Great Clarendon Street
Oxford OX2 6DP England

Oxford New York
Auckland Bangkok Buenos Aires Cape Town Chennai
Dar es Salaam Delhi Hong Kong Istanbul Karachi
Kolkata Kuala Lumpur Madrid Melbourne Mexico City
Mumbai Nairobi São Paulo Shanghai Taipei
Tokyo Toronto

OXFORD is a trademark of Oxford University Press.

ISBN 0-19-436773-8

Copyright © 2003 Oxford University Press

Editorial Manager: Janet Aitchison
Associate Editor: Kim Steiner
Associate Production Editor: Katya MacDonald
Art Director: Lynn Luchetti
Designer: Gail de Luca / Lyndall Culbertson
Art Buyer: Elizabeth Blomster
Production Manager: Shanta Persaud
Production Coordinator: Eve Wong

Printing (last digit): 10 9 8 7 6 5 4 3 2 1

Printed in Hong Kong.

Cover design by Silver Editions
Cover illustration by Rob Colvin
Illustrations by Wally Neibart, Stephanie O'Shaughnessy
Realia by Barbara Bastian, Susumu Kawabe

The publishers would like to thank the following for their
permission to reproduce photographs:

Ben & Jerry's/Associated Press; Bettman/Corbis; Byron
Collection/Museum of the City of New York; Christie's
Images/Corbis 2002 Artists Rights Society, New York/
ADAP, Paris; "Courtesy of the Edgar Allan Poe Museum,
Richmond, Virginia"; Furnari Jason/Corbis SYGMA;
Rob Gage/FPG; John Hill/Code Red 2002; Historical
Picture Archive/Corbis; Paul Howell/Liaison; Hulton-
Deutsch Collection/Corbis; Kimbell Art Museum/Corbis;
Charles & Josette Lenars/Corbis; James Leynse/Corbis; A.
Franco/The New York Times; Ben Margot/Associated Press;
Scala/Art Resource, NY; Herb Snitzer; Keren Su/Corbis;
John H. Tarbell/Corbis

The publishers would like to thank the following for their help:
p. 42 "Teen-Agers and Sex Roles." a New York Times/CBS
Poll from *The New York Times,* July 11, 1994. From the
article "Poll of Teen-Agers: Battle of the Sexes on Roles
in Family" by Tamar Lewin. Copyright © 1994 by The New
York Times Co. Reprinted by permission.

p. 46 "The Gender Gap" graph (Blau and Kahn) from
"Schools Brief: The War Between the Sexes." © 1994
The Economist Newspaper Group, Inc. Reprinted with
permission. Further reproduction prohibited.
www.economist.com.

p. 58–60 "Best Time to Be Alive; No Time Like the Past"
from *The New York Times Magazine,* April 18, 1999.
Reprinted with changes, by permission from Russell Baker,
Thomas Cahill, Ann Douglas, Elaine Pagels, Orlando
Patterson, Jonathan Spence, and The New York Times Co.

p. 78–79 Excerpt from *Summerhill: A Radical Approach to
Childrearing* by A.S. Neill. © 1960 by Mrs. E.M. Neil and
Zöe Readhead. Abridged and reprinted by permission.

p. 103 "Epworth Sleepiness Scale" by Dr. M.W. Johns,
Director, Epworth Sleep Center. Reprinted with permission
from Dr. Johns.

p. 106 "2000 Omnibus Sleep in America Poll." © 2000 The
National Sleep Foundation. Reprinted by permission.

p. 120–121 Vámos, Miklós. "How I'll Become an
American" from *The New York Times,* April 17, 1989.
Reproduced, with changes, by kind permission of the author.

p. 140–141 Navarro, Mireya. "For Parents, One Size
Doesn't Fit All in Bilingual Education" from *The New York
Times,* February 24, 2001. Copyright © 2001 by the New
York Times Co. Reprinted, with changes, by permission.

p. 157–158 Smith, Nora. "A Prayer for My Grandmother"
from *The Maryland Poetry Review* (#16/1997). Reproduced
by kind permission of the author.

p. 207 Chawla, Dipika. "The Tell-Tale Heart." *SCOPE,*
April 9, 2001. Reproduced by kind permission of the author.

Trademarks used in this text are the sole property of their
respective owners.

AUTHOR ACKNOWLEDGEMENTS

Our thanks go to Amy Cooper for embarking on this journey with us and for all the help and encouragement she has given us. We are grateful to Janet Aitchison for her expression of confidence in our work and for her professional insight at every stage of the creative process. We are very fortunate to have had a wonderful editor, Kim Steiner, whose dedication, sensitivity, and vision guided this project to its successful conclusion.

Our sincere thanks also go to Katya MacDonald, Elizabeth Blomster, and Gail de Luca for their essential contributions to this project.

We thank our colleagues at the Department of Language and Cognition at Eugenio Maria de Hostos Community College and the American Language Program at Columbia University for their professional support and friendship.

Finally, we remember our students, from whom we continue to learn every day and who remain in our hearts our true teachers.

In loving memory of my father, Sidney Elias Cohen, who expected great things of me.

Robert F. Cohen

To my mother, Sylvia Sondak Miller, my best friend, and my daughter Ariana, my inspiration.

Judy L. Miller

REASON TO WRITE

STRATEGIES FOR SUCCESS IN ACADEMIC WRITING

Introduction

Writing in one's own language is difficult enough. Imagine how much more daunting a task it is for students to write in a second language. If the weight of writer's block does not inhibit their impulse to move forward with a writing assignment, their insecurity with the language and its particular writing culture might make them stare at the blank page with trepidation. ESL/EFL teachers thus have a dual challenge: Not only must they help the most reticent and timid writers overcome a potentially crippling writing phobia, but they must also instill in their students the confidence needed to translate their thoughts into correct and acceptable English. The communicative approach that we use in the *Reason to Write* series will help teachers achieve this end.

Even though the writing product is an expression of one's individuality and personality, it is important to remember that writing is also a social endeavor, a way of communicating with others, informing them, persuading them, and debating with them. In our attempt to provide guidelines, strategies, and practice in writing for university, college, community college, and high school ESL/EFL students who are preparing for the academic demands of all disciplines in higher education, we want them to realize that they are not writing in a vacuum. They have a voice, and what they write will elicit a reaction from others. Therefore, in our books writing is an active communicative/social process that involves discussion, interaction with teachers, group work, pair work, and peer evaluation. Through these collaborative experiences, students come to recognize their unique strengths while cultivating their critical-thinking skills and becoming more effective writers.

Content-based themes that speak to both the hearts and minds of students are the key to realizing our goal. Writing can develop only where there is meaning; it cannot be an empty exercise in form. And meaning cannot be understood unless students are given intellectually challenging and emotionally appealing material that generates their enthusiasm. Because all instruction in grammar, vocabulary, and rhetorical styles is presented in relation to a theme, each unit provides a seamless path from reading to thinking to writing—from the preparatory stages of writing to the completion of a final composition. Working with one theme, the whole class experiences the same problem or issue together so students benefit from the security of shared discussion and exploration. As a result, writers are not left to suffer alone with the blank page. At the same time, students are given several writing options within each theme so that there is ample opportunity for individual expression.

Content-based themes also encourage the kind of critical thinking that students are expected to do across the curriculum in a college or university.

Because many English-language learners may lack some of the analytical skills needed to do academic work, we provide them with experience in analyzing ideas, making inferences, supporting opinions, understanding points of view, and writing for different audiences. As students "reason to write," they practice the skills and strategies that are vital for academic success, and they have an opportunity to write on a wide variety of themes that reflect the academic curriculum.

There are five main sections in each unit:

I. Fluency Practice: Freewriting

All units begin with an unstructured writing task in which students can freely express their thoughts and share them with a partner, without worrying about grammar or spelling. In this section, students explore the theme of the unit by drawing on their own knowledge and ideas. As a result, they enter subsequent discussions with more self-assurance.

II. Reading for Writing

In order to develop as a writer, one must be a reader. Therefore, each unit contains a provocative reading passage followed by a series of writing activities that culminate in the main writing task of the unit. In this section, students consider the meaning of the reading and they work with the vocabulary and syntactic forms needed for discussing and writing.

III. Prewriting Activities

This section prepares the students for the main writing task by developing their interpretive skills. They must "read between the lines"—infer the motives of individuals in various scenarios and write from different points of view. They are also asked to write short opinions of their own—and learn to summarize group discussions. As they complete these small writing tasks, students give and receive immediate feedback through ongoing dialogue with a partner or group, building confidence for the main writing task in the next section.

IV. Structured Writing Focus

When students reach the main writing task, they realize that all their work in previous sections has prepared them for this central writing assignment. Because we feel that students should be given choices, we have provided an alternative writing task.

In this section of the unit, students are guided through a series of steps that will lead them to the successful completion of the writing task. In the first book of the *Reason to Write* series, students learn the rudiments of writing a well-developed paragraph. In this second book, they acquire the skill needed to write well-developed essays. In Unit 1, students review paragraph unity and coherence. In Units 2 and 3, they write three-paragraph essays. In Units 6 through 10, students write five-paragraph essays. Students practice writing introductions and conclusions, thesis statements, transitional sentences, and supplying details. They negotiate tasks as varied as writing a personal narrative, interpreting the language of graphs, and writing five-paragraph essays, such as cause and effect, satirical, argumentative, and comparison-contrast. At the end of the second book of this series, students respond to a final challenge: writing a literary analysis of a famous short story. This last writing assignment brings to light the exciting writing opportunities that students can look forward to in their continued study of English.

To give students the support they need to accomplish the writing tasks, we provide a model for them to follow. The model is on a topic that is similar to the writing topic. Students then work through the brainstorming process and do exercises that help them prepare a first draft. After writing their first draft, they read it to a partner or a small group of students. In this way, peer evaluation becomes a regular part of the writing process and the class becomes a "writing workshop" through which the writing process is demystified. This approach also shows students how to look critically at their own work. Our guidelines for peer work ensure that this is a positive experience, a prelude but not a substitute for feedback from the teacher.

After writing a second draft, students are ready to proofread their work. At this point, the unit focuses on grammar. Students work through various editing exercises that focus on at least one grammar point that is central to the particular writing task and on another grammar point that is a general stumbling block for students at this level. After completing these grammar exercises and editing their second draft, students are ready to write their final draft.

V. Additional Writing Opportunities

We believe that students can perfect their writing skills only by writing a great deal. Therefore, in this section we give them the opportunity to write on a wide variety of additional stimulating topics. However, this time they are writing without our step-by-step guidance. As students learn to avail themselves of this additional writing practice in each unit, they will eventually develop the skills and confidence they need to become independent writers.

In conclusion, the *Reason to Write* series integrates the insights of whole-language learning, writing across the curriculum, and writing workshops. These books were also written with the knowledge that no textbook can come to life and be effective without the creative contributions of the teachers and students who use it. We hope that you and your students will develop a strong connection with the material in this book and thus form a bond with us as you explore the writing process. We would appreciate any suggestions or comments you may have. You can write to us in care of Oxford University Press, ESL Department, 198 Madison Avenue, New York, New York 10016-4314.

Robert F. Cohen and Judy L. Miller

CONTENTS

Editing focus:
    subordinate clauses
    because / because of
    logical connectors
    fragments
    run-on sentences and comma splices

UNIT 7   HOW I'LL BECOME AN AMERICAN

Writing a Satirical Essay

Reading:
    "How I'll Become an American," by Miklós Vámos
    (from *The New York Times*)

Writing practice:
    using text references to support your opinion
    making inferences
    understanding puns
    writing humorous details

Editing focus:
    causatives
    -ing/-ed adjective endings

UNIT 8   FOR AND AGAINST BILINGUAL EDUCATION

Writing an Argumentative Essay

Reading:
    "Bilingual Education: Parents' Views" (from *The New York Times*)

Writing practice:
    defending your point of view
    refuting opposing views
    conceding to an opposing view and replying
    using the language of concession

Editing focus:
    present unreal conditionals
    connectors: *despite / despite the fact that* and *although / even though*

WRITING A PERSONAL NARRATIVE

In this unit you will practice:
- taking notes and summarizing a discussion
- developing paragraph unity

Editing focus:
- habitual past vs. simple past
- pronouns and possessive adjectives
- indentation
- capitalization
- quotation marks

 ## Fluency Practice: Freewriting

Look at the picture. What is the relationship between these two people? How do you think they feel about each other?

Write for ten minutes. Try to express yourself as well as you can. Don't worry about mistakes. Share your writing with a partner.

II ▶ Reading for Writing

Frederick Bailey (1817–1895) was born into slavery in the South of the United States. He escaped to freedom in the North when he was a young man. There he changed his name from Bailey to Douglass, in part to hide from slave catchers. Frederick Douglass became a speaker and writer and started his own antislavery newspaper. The following four paragraphs are adapted excerpts from his *Narrative of the Life of Frederick Douglass* (1845), which he wrote to tell people about the horrors of slavery.

NARRATIVE OF THE LIFE OF FREDERICK DOUGLASS

I

My mother was named Harriet Bailey. She was the daughter of Isaac and Betsey Bailey. My father was a white man. People whispered that my master
5 was my father, but I don't know if this is true. My mother and I were separated when I was but an infant. It is the custom in Maryland to send the mother to work at another farm before the child
10 is 12 months old. The child is put under the care of an old woman, too old for field labor. My mother made her journeys to see me at night, traveling 12 miles on foot, after her day's work. She
15 would lie down and get me to sleep, but long before I woke, she was gone. Death soon ended what little communication we could have had while she lived, and with it, all her hardships and suffering. She died when I was seven years old on one of my master's farms near Lee's Mill.

II

I was probably eight when I left Colonel Lloyd's plantation and was sent
20 to Baltimore to live with my master's brother-in-law Mr. Auld. During this time, I began to learn how to read and write. My mistress was a kind and pious[1] woman who had never owned a slave before. Before her marriage, she had made a living from her work. She had been a weaver.[2]

---

1. *pious:* religious, having a deep respect for God and religion
2. *weaver:* a person who earns a living by making cloth from thread

She treated me the way she supposed that one human being should treat another. She very kindly began to teach me the ABCs. But her husband found out what she was doing and told her not to teach me anymore. It was against the law to teach a slave to read. He said, "A slave should only know how to obey his master, nothing more. If you teach him to read, he will be discontented and unhappy, and he will be of no use as a slave." My mistress then began to obey her husband. She finally became more violent in her opposition to my reading than her husband. But, from that moment, I understood the pathway[3] to freedom.

III

When I was sent on errands, I always took my book. I used to carry bread with me. Enough of it was always in the house and I was always welcome to it. I had more bread than some of the poor white children in the neighborhood. This bread I used to give to these hungry children and they, in return, would give me the valuable bread of knowledge. With their help, I finally succeeded in learning to read. I would sometimes talk with them about slavery. I would say, "You will be free as soon as you are 21 years old, but I am a slave for life. Do I not have the same right to be free as you?" These words used to trouble them. They would express for me the greatest sympathy and console[4] me with the hope that something would occur so that I might be free one day.

IV

The more I read, the more I began to detest[5] my enslavers. They were just a band of successful robbers who had left their homes, gone to Africa, stolen us from our homes, and in a strange land, reduced us to slavery. I hated them as the meanest and most evil of men. I would sometimes feel that learning had been a bad thing for me and not a good thing. It had given me the understanding of my terrible condition, but not the remedy.[6] I often wished I was a beast, anything, just to make me stop thinking. I often found myself regretting my own existence and wishing myself dead. Without the hope of being free, I have no doubt that I would have killed myself or done something that would have made others kill me. One day I got one of the city newspapers. I read an article about people from the North praying for the end of slavery.[7] From this time on, the light broke upon me. I decided to run away to the North.

---

3. *pathway:* a road
4. *console:* to show sympathy for someone who is sad and to help make him or her feel better
5. *detest:* to hate
6. *remedy:* a cure, a solution to a problem
7. Douglass read about abolitionism, a movement of both Whites and African Americans who wanted to end slavery. William Lloyd Garrison was a famous abolitionist who published the newspaper *The Liberator.*

A. General Understanding

Match the incomplete sentences with the verb phrases in the box to make true statements about the reading. More than one ending may match. One ending does not match any sentence.

1. Douglass's mother . . .   b,

2. An old woman . . .   _____

3. Mrs. Auld started to teach
   Douglass to read, but she . . .   _____

4. Douglass gave bread to poor white
   children so that they . . .   _____

5. After he learned to read, Douglass . . .   _____

> a. would let him see their books.
> b. took care of him until he was almost one year old.
> c. beat him very badly.
> d. walked 12 miles and back to see him.
> e. died when he was seven.
> f. stopped because it was against the law.
> g. decided to run away.
> h. wished he were dead.
> i. took care of Douglass because she was too old to work in the fields.

Answer these questions in your own words. Write in your notebook. Share your answers with a partner.

1. Why did Douglass begin his story by talking about his family?

2. How did Mrs. Auld's attitude toward Douglass change?

3. Why did Douglass want to die?

4. What made him change his mind?

5. What were your feelings when you read Douglass's writing?

Look back at the paragraphs from Frederick Douglass's Narrative *on pages 2–3. What main idea(s) does each paragraph illustrate? Write your answers in your notebook. Compare your answers with a partner's.*

In the first paragraph, Douglass describes his family origins and the first years of his life.

B. Working with Language

1. Adjectives Describing Behavior

With a partner, write the correct adjective from this list to answer each of the questions below.

childish	fearful	manipulative
clever	foolish	obedient
courageous	generous	practical
cruel	helpless	sympathetic

How would you describe people who . . .

1. always do what they are told? _____

2. react to a situation with common sense? _____

3. are nervous and afraid? _____

4. behave in an immature way? _____

5. try to understand the feelings of others? _____

6. behave in an intelligent way? _____

7. help others without expecting anything in return? _____

8. influence other people to do or think what they want them to? _____

9. are brave and save the lives of others? _____

10. act without thinking about the consequences? _____

11. are weak and can't fight back? _____

12. treat others in a mean and harsh way? _____

2. Describing Characters

Write adjectives from the list on the previous page to describe these people. You may need to use more than one adjective for each person. Discuss your answers with a partner.

1. Harriet Bailey: <u>courageous,</u>

2. Mrs. Auld: _____

3. Mr. Auld: _____

4. Frederick Douglass: _____

5. The poor white children: _____

3. Identifying Nouns and Adjectives

A **noun** is a person, place, thing, or idea.

Douglass's **cleverness** helped him to escape **slavery** in the **South.**
       NOUN   NOUN   NOUN

An **adjective** describes a noun.

Frederick Douglass was a **courageous hero.**
                              ADJECTIVE   NOUN

These lists show adjectives with their corresponding noun forms. Complete the paragraphs on the next page with the appropriate adjective or noun. Compare your answers with a partner's.

Adjectives		Nouns
childish	⟶	childishness
clever	⟶	cleverness
courageous	⟶	courage
cruel	⟶	cruelty
fearful	⟶	fear
foolish	⟶	foolishness
generous	⟶	generosity
helpless	⟶	helplessness
manipulative	⟶	manipulation
obedient	⟶	obedience
practical	⟶	practicality
sympathetic	⟶	sympathy

A group of slaves outside their log cabin lodging

Life under Slavery

It is not hard to imagine how **h**elpless____ Frederick Douglass felt as a
child condemned to slavery. Because he had no power over his life, he was
forced to think of **c**_____ ways to escape slavery. The first way was
to learn to read. In return for giving his master's bread to white children,
Douglass gained valuable knowledge about the world he lived in from
them. The white children obviously had a **p**_____ interest in trading
their knowledge for bread: they were hungry. But they also may have
understood the great **c**_____ it took for Douglass to live in such a
c_____ system. It would be interesting to know what happened to
these children in their later lives. Did their **s**_____ for this slave
child make them hate slavery? Or was this experience just a **f**_____
adventure that they quickly forgot?

Historians believe that the majority of white people in the South owned
no slaves at all. There are estimates that only 5 percent of all white
Southerners owned enough slaves (more than 20) to make a plantation.

But all white Southerners were taught to be **o**_____ and accept
slavery as the law. Were they victims of **m**_____ on the part of the
big landowners? Did white people who didn't own slaves accept slavery
out of a love of their homeland or out of a **f**_____ of the slaves?
Perhaps both these factors played a role in the continuation of slavery. But
the consequence of slavery was war. In 1861 the Civil War began—the
bloodiest war in American history.

III ▸ Prewriting Activities

A. Point-of-View Writing

*Read the situations on the opposite page. Choose one and write a letter as if you
were a character from Douglass's* Narrative. *Write your letter in your notebook
using the style below to help you.*

Dear _____,
_____
_____
_____
_____
_____
_____
_____
_____

Love,

_____

Situation 1

You are Mr. or Mrs. Auld. Describe in a letter to a friend what happened when Frederick Douglass began learning to read. Explain how you feel about this and why.

Situation 2

You are one of the young people who let Frederick Douglass use your books. Write a letter to your parents explaining why you helped a slave learn to read and how you feel about what you did.

Exchange letters with a partner. Read your partner's letter and write a reply to it in your notebook.

Reply 1

If your partner wrote as Mr. or Mrs. Auld, write a reply as a friend.

Reply 2

If your partner wrote as a young person who helped Frederick Douglass learn to read, write a reply as one of the young person's parents.

Exchange these letters of reply with your partner. What was your partner's main idea? Did any part of your partner's reply surprise you? What was the best part of the letter?

B. Open for Discussion

Discuss these questions in a small group. Each member of the group should choose one question and take notes on the group's answers. Notes do not have to be written in complete sentences. Use the model on the next page to help you take notes.

1. Consider the statement, "Work is freedom." Would Frederick Douglass agree or disagree with this statement? Do you think work is freedom?

2. Did Frederick Douglass think that education is the pathway to freedom? Do you agree? Is education enough to make someone free?

3. How are childhood and slavery similar to or different from each other?

4. Who is made less human by slavery, the master or the slave? Explain your answer.

Discussion	Notes
Student 1: I think FD would not agree with this quote. The slaves were forced to work. There was no freedom in it.	**Student 1:** FD would not agree with quote. No freedom. Slaves forced to work.
Student 2: Work could be freedom if you choose it and if you love the work you do. Of course, in FD's case, this was not the situation.	**Student 2:** work = freedom if you choose the work and love it. For FD no choice = no freedom.

C. A Summary of Opinions

A **summary** is a short statement of the main ideas from a discussion or piece of writing.

Write a four to five sentence summary of your group's discussion on the question you selected. Use your notes and the model below to help you write it.

MODEL SUMMARY OF GROUP DISCUSSION ON QUESTION 1

In our group, we all agreed that Frederick Douglass would not think that work is freedom because as a slave he was forced to work. However, one person in the group thought that work could be freedom if you choose the work you do. Another person disagreed because most people just work in order to live. This person felt that freedom meant having a lot of leisure time: the right to be lazy!

When you have finished writing your summary, read it aloud to your group. Make sure that you have correctly recorded the opinions of the different students in the group.

IV Structured Writing Focus

Write a personal narrative in one or two paragraphs. Each paragraph should have at least five sentences. Tell a story about your past that describes your personality and the people around you at that time. Explain how your life experiences have influenced you.

ALTERNATIVE TASK: Write one or two paragraphs about a problem you had to overcome or a decision that you had to make. Write in the first person using the pronoun *I*.

A. Starting to Write

1. Brainstorming

Most writers find that a writing task is easier to begin if they **brainstorm**—think about all of their ideas on the topic—before they start.

Experiment with these brainstorming techniques. Then use the ones that work best for you to write your paragraphs.

TECHNIQUES FOR BRAINSTORMING

- Some writers just think about what they want to write about.

- Other writers prefer to talk about their ideas with a friend or a colleague.

- Some people speak into a tape recorder because they find it easier to say their ideas in private first and then write them.

- Many people write all the ideas they can think of, freely—without stopping—in notes.

- Others prefer to write organized outlines.

---

2. Questions to Get You Started

Write brainstorming notes for your first draft in your notebook. Consider these questions to help you write.

FOR THE MAIN AND ALTERNATIVE TASKS

What aspects of your personality do you want to write about? Are you intelligent? talented? sensitive? sympathetic? hard-working?

Another aspect: _____

What period in your life do you want to write about? childhood? growing up? school years? today?

Another period: _____

Do you want to write about any of these subjects: your family origins? learning something important? overcoming a problem or sadness? choosing your future life?

Another subject: _____

B. Preparing the First Draft

Choosing Ideas for Paragraph Unity

Every paragraph of an essay must have **unity**, that is, a paragraph must have one main idea, and every sentence in the paragraph must be relevant to that main idea.

Read these brainstorming notes that were written by a student applying to a business program. Then read the paragraph she wrote from them about what she learned from her summer job. Compare the notes with the paragraph and discuss with a partner why some of the notes were crossed out.

Brainstorming Notes

~~My family is sort of poor~~

Work over the summer

Met my boyfriend there

Realized business career is my goal

Toy department

~~Trouble with grades in science~~

Store experience: learn a lot from salespeople

Work hard

Don't waste time

Think of the customer first

~~Show manager he couldn't push me around~~

Money from commissions

Got promotion

Business in My Future

From the time I was in high school, I knew that business was the career for me. At 16 I worked in the toy department of Sears, where I earned a 10 percent commission on everything I sold in addition to my salary. That was all the motivation I needed! I always went out of my way to help customers because I realized that if I worked hard, I would succeed. I did. Even though I was still in high school, I earned more in commission than many full-time employees. I also learned the importance of making the best use of my time. On the weekends I slept in. I saw that the most productive salespeople made use of every minute. I did the same, and my boss promoted me because of my efficiency; also, he saw that I was ready for new responsibilities. Unfortunately, a business slump has caused many store closings in our area. My job at the toy department convinced me that I have the energy and ambition to make a career in business, and that's why I want to go to business school.

Read the above paragraph again for paragraph unity. Then answer these questions on the lines provided.

1. What is the main idea of the paragraph?

   _____

   _____

2. Which two sentences do not support the main idea and should be removed?

   _____

   _____

Now read over your own brainstorming notes and select sentences to write a first draft of your paragraph(s). Make sure that each paragraph has one idea.

C. Revising the First Draft

We revise the first draft of an essay to clarify ideas, further explain them, and organize them effectively. Revisions improve the content of an essay. Reading your work aloud to another student before showing it to a teacher can be helpful because you can hear what you have written and get **feedback**—comments and suggestions—from your peer.

Read these instructions for peer evaluation. Then during your evaluation, complete the Checklist for Revising the First Draft that follows.

INSTRUCTIONS FOR PEER EVALUATION

1. Read your first draft to a partner and allow your partner to see your paragraph(s).Then listen to your partner read his or her personal narrative and read it yourself.

2. Write down the detail that is the most interesting to you.

3. Do not comment on grammar at this time unless an error makes the ideas difficult to understand.

4. Write your comments as suggestions. Your partner will decide whether to make changes or not. Be a sympathetic listener and stress the positive.

CHECKLIST FOR REVISING THE FIRST DRAFT

When you listen to your partner's essay and when you discuss your own, keep these questions in mind:

1. Is the main idea of each paragraph clear?

2. Does every sentence in each paragraph relate to the main idea of that paragraph?

3. Does anything need more explanation?

4. Is the story written in the first person using the pronoun *I* ?

5. Do you need to add more adjectives to describe yourself or other people better?

*Now write a **second draft** that includes all additions and changes.*

D. Editing the Second Draft

After you have written a second draft, proofread your work for any errors and correct them. These guidelines and exercises should help.

1. Habitual Past vs. Simple Past

Study these sentences. Then answer the questions below.

   a. I watch the children.

   b. I watched the children.

   c. I used to watch the children.

1. Which two sentences show that the action happened in the past?

2. Which sentence shows that the action is happening in the present?

3. Which sentence suggests that the action happened many times in the past, not only once?

HABITUAL PAST WITH USED TO AND WOULD

Used to describes a past condition or an action that happened many times in the past. The condition or action is not true now.

used to + base form of verb
I **used to carry** bread with me every day.

The habitual past is also expressed by the past conditional *would* in formal writing.

She **would** lie down and get me to sleep.

Write five sentences that describe what you used to do when you were a child. Use the habitual past. Share your sentences with a partner.

When I was a child, I used to . . .

1. _____

2. _____

3. _____

4. _____

5. _____

CONTRAST OF THE HABITUAL PAST WITH THE SIMPLE PAST

The simple past can be used to describe both an action that happened only once in the past and an action that happened many times.

I **used to carry** bread with me every day.
HABITUAL PAST TENSE

This happened many times in the past, not only once.

I **carried** bread with me.
SIMPLE PAST TENSE

This happened either once or many times in the past.

Incorrect
In 1861, the Civil War **used to begin.**

The verb cannot be in the habitual past because a war can begin only once.

Correct
In 1861, the Civil War **began.**

Read this paragraph. Write the correct form of the verb: habitual past with used to *or simple past on the lines provided. Some verbs can be in both tenses.*

Before 1954, most public schools in the South of the United States

_____ (used to be / were) segregated. Segregation meant
                1

that racial groups were separated. In the South at that time, white children

and African American children _____ (used to go / went)
                                            2

to different schools. They _____ (used to learn / learned)
                                      3

their school subjects without coming into contact with one another.

Everything _____ (used to start / started) to change when
                        4

the Supreme Court _____ (used to decide / decided) in 1954
                                5

that segregation was unconstitutional.[1] People _____
                                                                          6

(used to realize / realized) that children of all races had to learn how to live

with one another.

_____

1. *unconstitutional:* against the U.S. Constitution (for more information, see Unit 2, p. 26)

2. Avoiding Repetition: Pronouns and Possessive Adjectives

You can improve your writing style by avoiding repetition of nouns. Use **pronouns** and **possessive adjectives** to replace nouns after the first time they appear.

Compare the sentences on the left with those from Douglass's Narrative *on the right. Then complete the exercise that follows.*

CORRECT BUT POOR STYLE	CORRECT AND GOOD STYLE
My mother made her journeys to see me at night. **My mother** would lie down and get me to sleep, but long before I woke, **my mother** was gone.	**My mother** made her journeys to see me at night. **She** would lie down and get me to sleep, but long before I woke, **she** was gone.
The slaves suffer from a lack of sleep; for when **the slaves'** work in the field is done, many of **the slaves'** sleeping hours are used up in preparing for the next work day.	**The slaves** suffer from a lack of sleep; for when **their** work in the field is done, many of **their** sleeping hours are used up in preparing for the next work day.

These sentences are additional excerpts from Frederick Douglass's Narrative. *Find the repeated nouns and change them to pronouns and possessive adjectives. Do not change the noun the first time it appears. Compare your sentences with a partner's.*

1. Very little communication ever took place between my mother and me. My mother died when I was seven years old. I was not allowed to be present during my mother's illness, at my mother's death, or at my mother's burial. My mother was gone before I knew anything about it.

2. I have had two masters. My first master's last name was Anthony. I do not remember my first master's first name. My first master was not considered a rich slaveholder. My first master owned two or three farms and about thirty slaves.

3. Mr. and Mrs. Auld were both at home, and Mr. and Mrs. Auld met me at the door with Mr. and Mrs. Auld's little son, Thomas.

3. Style Rules

It is important to follow the rules on indentation, capitalization, and quotation marks when you edit your writing.

In academic writing, paragraphs start with an indentation a few spaces from the left-hand page margin. Look at the indentation in the example paragraph below.

> The more I read, the more I began to detest my enslavers. They were just a band of successful robbers who had left their homes, gone to Africa, stolen us from our homes, and in a strange land, reduced us to slavery. I hated them as the meanest and most evil of men. I would sometimes feel that learning had been a bad thing for me and not a good thing. It had given me the understanding of my terrible condition, but not the remedy.

The first letter of every sentence must be capitalized.

I used to carry bread with me.

The first letter of each word in a title must be capitalized, with the exception of short prepositions and articles.

Narrative of the Life of Frederick Douglass

The first letter of the name of every person and place must be capitalized.

Person: Frederick Douglass
Place: Baltimore, Maryland

The names of nationalities, wars, official organizations, days, and months must be capitalized.

Nationality: American
War: Civil War
Official organization: Congress
Dates: Monday, March 4, 1861

Quotation marks (". . . .") are needed when you use the exact words that a person has said or written. Place the second quotation mark after a period, comma, question mark, or exclamation point.

Frederick Douglass wrote, "My mother was named Harriet Bailey."
"My mother was named Harriet Bailey," said Frederick Douglass.

Working with a partner, add the correct indentation, capitalization, and quotation marks where necessary to the essay below.

frederick douglass, an american hero

frederick douglass played an extraordinary role in american history. He was born a slave in maryland in 1817. he never saw his brother and two sisters until he was seven years old. He later wrote in this *Narrative*, Slavery made us strangers. At 21, Douglass worked on the docks in Baltimore. from there, he managed to escape from slavery using the identity papers of a free black sailor. He then went to new york city where he married ann murray, a free black woman whom he had first met in baltimore. he chose a new name: douglass from sir walter scott's novel, *The lady of the lake*. in his new life, frederick douglass became an important abolitionist. he helped slaves escape to the north by means of the Underground Railroad. in 1847 he began to publish his own newspaper called *The North Star*. this was the name of the star that escaping slaves followed north in search of freedom. In his newspaper, douglass fought for justice for the oppressed. at the first Women's Rights Convention in 1848, he demanded that women be allowed to vote. During the civil war, he pressured president lincoln to allow black people to fight in the Union Army for their freedom. Douglass's sons fought among the black troops. Douglass later became u.s. ambassador to haiti, the world's first black republic. he also became a leader of howard university, the first university for African Americans in the united states. Frederick douglass is an American hero.

E. Preparing the Final Draft

Reread your second draft and correct any errors you find. Put a check (✔) in each space as you edit for these points. Then write your corrected final version.

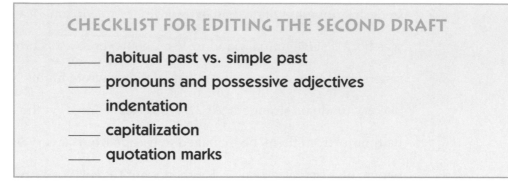

CHECKLIST FOR EDITING THE SECOND DRAFT

_____ habitual past vs. simple past

_____ pronouns and possessive adjectives

_____ indentation

_____ capitalization

_____ quotation marks

 V ## Additional Writing Opportunities

Choose one of the following topics to write a paragraph about. Check for paragraph unity and practice the editing skills you have learned. Use some of the new vocabulary from this chapter.

1. Write a formal personal narrative in which you introduce yourself to a future employer. You can choose a story about your past working experience or about your studies. Explain why you would be a good employee and why the company should hire you. Describe your energy, enthusiasm, and skills.

2. Write a formal personal narrative for an application to a four-year college or business school. You can tell a story that will show your desire for higher education or your ability to overcome obstacles. Describe your personality and talents.

3. Write an informal personal narrative introducing yourself to an on-line community on the Internet. Your narrative, written for E-mail, should communicate the interests that you wish to share with others.

4. Have you ever experienced a lack of freedom? Describe this experience, how it felt, and whether you were able to change it.

5. Have you ever experienced prejudice? Write about your experience or your thoughts about prejudice directed against race, religion, nationality, or gender.

2 WHAT'S YOUR VERDICT?

**WRITING A
THREE-PARAGRAPH
OPINION ESSAY**

In this unit you will practice:
- writing introductions, thesis statements, and conclusions

Editing focus:
- active and passive voice
- transitive and intransitive verbs

I Fluency Practice: Freewriting

Justice systems determine whether people are guilty or not guilty of a crime. What do you think the statue above suggests about justice? What do the scale and sword represent? Why is the statue of Justice blindfolded? Do you think the law brings us justice? Why or why not?

Write for ten minutes. Try to express yourself as well as you can. Don't worry about mistakes. Share your writing with a partner.

II   Reading for Writing

This reading is based on a true story that happened several years ago in the United States.

The Case of Leroy Strachan

A 62-year-old New York resident has been arrested for a murder that took place 45 years ago in Miami, Florida.

Mr. Strachan, who pronounces his name "Strawn," was arrested outside a building in SoHo in New York City, where he had been working as an elevator operator for 21 years. He is accused of being part of a group of young men responsible for the death of John Milledge, a Miami policeman.

Officer Milledge was chasing a group of young men out of a park 45 years ago when he was killed by a single rifle shot. Prosecutors in Miami said that Leroy Strachan was a suspect at the time of the killing, but that they did not have enough evidence to charge him at that time. Just recently, however, a Miami woman who claims she saw the crime came forward to say that Strachan had fired the shot. The woman said her guilty conscience finally made her go to the police.

Friends and neighbors of Strachan, even officials who investigated the case, all agree that he led a quiet, churchgoing life since he moved to New York the day after the shooting. According to Strachan's defense lawyer, William Kunstler, Strachan raised three sons, held a steady job, and never got so much as a traffic ticket or had any brush with the law[1] before his arrest. Mr. Kunstler also said that Strachan has never considered himself a fugitive from justice[2] because he went back to Florida up to six times every year since the incident to visit his mother. Mr. Strachan's niece, Deborah Clear, made the following statement: "We feel the courts[3] lack compassion. If these people knew my uncle, they would let him go. If there is a perfect person, it is Leroy Strachan."

Although many people in Florida expressed sympathy for Mr. Strachan and would like state officials to drop the charges,[4] police groups and Officer Milledge's family want Mr. Strachan to be brought to trial. Even though Florida has the death penalty,[5] prosecutors are unlikely to seek it in this case, primarily because the victim's family has asked them not to do so.

---

1. *brush with the law:* trouble with the police
2. *fugitive from justice:* a person hiding from the police
3. *courts:* the legal system
4. *drop the charges:* stop legal action against someone
5. *the death penalty:* the execution of criminals by the government; also called capital punishment

What do you think? Should Leroy Strachan be put on trial in Florida for a crime he is accused of committing 45 years ago?

A. General Understanding

Identifying People, Places, and Things

Write a sentence for each of these people, places, or things explaining how they relate to the reading. Share your answers with a partner.

1. Crime

   A 62-year-old man named Leroy Strachan has been arrested for a crime that took place 45 years ago.

2. Rifle

3. John Milledge

4. A Miami woman

5. William Kunstler

6. Florida

7. New York

B. Working with Language

1. Learning Legal Vocabulary

Match the words defined below with the locations of the participants in this diagram of an American courtroom.

___a___ 1. **defendant:** the person who is on trial for a crime she or he is accused of committing.

_____ 2. **prosecutor:** the lawyer representing the government. This lawyer's job is to prove that the defendant is guilty.

_____ 3. **defense attorney:** the lawyer representing the accused person. This lawyer's job is to prove that the defendant is not guilty.

_____ 4. **jury:** the 12 people who decide whether the defendant is innocent or guilty. The jury listens to the witnesses, examines the evidence, and gives a verdict (decision). In a murder trial a verdict must be unanimous (all the jurors must agree on it).

_____ 5. **judge:** the legal expert who makes sure that legal procedure is followed in the courtroom. In jury trials the judge does not decide whether the defendant is innocent or guilty; the judge chooses the sentence (punishment).

_____ 6. **witness:** a person who has evidence, such as knowledge about the crime or the defendant. In court a witness must testify (make a formal statement to the jury and judge).

Working with a partner, use these words to fill in the blanks below.

defendant   defense attorney   evidence   judge   jury

prosecutor   sentence   unanimous   verdict   witnesses

Leroy Strachan, who was arrested for killing Officer Milledge 45 years ago, is now in police custody. If the state of Florida decides to try the court case, that is, bring the case to trial, William Kunstler, the _____,
                                                                                       1

will attempt to prove Strachan's innocence. He will argue the case against

the other lawyer, the state _____, who will attempt to
                               2

prove Strachan's guilt. The case will be heard by a _____
                                                        3

and a _____ of 12 people. The 12 jurors will examine all of
          4

the _____ and decide the defendant's innocence or guilt.
        5

The judge will make sure that all legal procedures are properly followed.

The _____ will testify about what they saw. Both lawyers
        6

will try to influence the jury's _____. In a murder trial,
                                    7

a verdict of guilty cannot be reached unless all of the jurors agree and the

decision is _____. If the _____ is
                8   9

convicted, the judge will decide Strachan's _____.
                                                10

2. Reading the U.S. Constitution

The U.S. Constitution is the supreme law of the United States of America. This means that no state or local governments can pass laws that conflict with the Constitution. The first ten amendments to the Constitution are known as the Bill of Rights.

Read this paragraph from the Bill of Rights that guarantees the right to a fair trial. Then match the words below from the Bill of Rights with their definitions. Compare your answers with a partner's.

*The trial of all crimes shall be by jury. In all criminal **prosecutions**, the accused shall enjoy the right to a **speedy** and **public** trial, by an **impartial** jury of the state and **district** where the crime was committed. The accused shall also enjoy the right **to be informed** of the reason for his arrest, **to be confronted with** the **witnesses** against him, to find witnesses in his favor, and to have the assistance of **counsel** for his defense.*

_d_ 1. prosecutions	a. quick, with no unnecessary delays
___ 2. speedy	b. fair, without prejudice
___ 3. public	c. to come face-to-face with someone (or something)
___ 4. impartial	d. criminal charges against a person in a court of law
___ 5. district	e. a lawyer
___ 6. to be informed	f. open for all to see, not in secret
___ 7. to be confronted with	g. people who have firsthand knowledge about the case or about the defendant
___ 8. witnesses	h. a unit of local government
___ 9. counsel	i. to have received information

III ▸ Prewriting Activities

A. Constitutional or Unconstitutional?

Working with a partner, read and discuss these legal actions. If the action follows the laws of the Constitution, check (✓) Constitutional. If it does not, check Unconstitutional. Refer to the quote from the Bill of Rights on the previous page to help you decide. Then explain your decision in your notebook.

1. The police arrest a man, handcuff him, and say, "You are coming with us. We are putting you in jail." The man remains in jail for two weeks without seeing anyone.

   Constitutional _____

   Unconstitutional _____

2. A woman is tried for robbing a grocery store. A jury decides she is guilty, and the judge sentences her to two years in prison. A few months after the trial, it is discovered that one of the jurors was a blood relative of the man who owned the grocery store.

   Constitutional _____

   Unconstitutional _____

3. A man is accused of killing someone in Montana. The Wyoming police find him living in their state. They arrest him. The state of Wyoming tries him, finds him guilty, and sends him to jail for life.

   Constitutional _____

   Unconstitutional _____

4. A young man is arrested for vandalism (destroying property). He is brought to trial in the district where the crime was committed, represented by a defense attorney, confronted with the witnesses, and found guilty by a jury of 12 men and women. The judge sentences him to three months in prison and a year of community service.

   Constitutional _____

   Unconstitutional _____

B. Point-of-View Writing

Read the situations below. In your notebook, write how you would feel about Strachan's case if you were each of the following people. Share your explanations with a partner.

1. You are a Miami police officer. Explain why you believe that Leroy Strachan should be put on trial.

   Leroy Strachan should be put on trial because . . .

2. You are a member of Leroy Strachan's family. Explain why you believe that Leroy Strachan should not be put on trial.

3. You are a member of the family of Officer Milledge, the victim. Explain why you believe that Leroy Strachan should not receive the death penalty.

4. You are one of Leroy Strachan's friends. Explain why you believe that Leroy Strachan will not be able to get a fair trial.

C. Open for Discussion

Discuss these questions in a small group.

1. What do you think the purpose of prisons should be:
   a. To separate dangerous criminals from the rest of the population?
   b. To punish criminals?
   c. To reform criminals and make them better citizens?

2. Should parents be held responsible for a crime committed by a child who is under the age of 18?

3. In many countries, the judge decides guilt or innocence, not the jury. Do you think that a legal expert such as a judge should decide the verdict, or the ordinary people on a jury? Explain your answer.

4. Many states in the United States impose the death penalty. Do you believe in capital punishment? Why or why not?

5. Do you think that the media should be allowed to put trials on TV? How is this good or bad for our society?

IV Structured Writing Focus

Write a three-paragraph opinion essay about the Strachan case. Leroy Strachan has admitted his involvement in the murder of Officer Milledge. He has lived a responsible life since the time when he committed this crime. Should he be sent to prison for a crime he committed 45 years ago?

ALTERNATIVE TASK: Many people serve their time in prison and are released, but they end up committing another crime and return to prison. Because of this, some critics believe that the criminal justice system does not function well. Write a three-paragraph essay on how the criminal justice system should be organized to work better.

A. Starting to Write

Brainstorming

Look back at your answers from the Prewriting Activities on pages 27–28 to start brainstorming for your essay. In your notebook, write notes for the task above that you have chosen. Consider these questions to help you write.

FOR THE MAIN TASK

Should a crime that happened a long time ago still be subject to trial? Can witnesses still have a reliable memory of past events? Does this make their evidence valid?

Do you think that prison is necessary to reform criminals? Or can a person change over time by himself or herself?

FOR THE ALTERNATIVE TASK

Should people who commit less serious crimes be given sentences other than prison? For example, house arrest (confinement to one's house), community service, parole, a rehabilitation program, or paying a heavy tax. What types of crimes, if any, should receive these lighter punishments?

Should prison sentences be longer for violent criminals so that they cannot commit repeat crimes? For example, should violent criminals be imprisoned for life without parole (chance of release)? Will this prevent crime?

B. Preparing the First Draft

1. Essay Structure: Writing Introductions, Body Paragraphs, and Conclusions

Read this essay. Then answer the questions that follow with a partner.

Education and Criminals

Introduction →
"No man is an island," wrote the English poet John Donne. We are not alone in this world, and what we do has an effect on others. In fact, what we do for prisoners will affect our lives as well as theirs. If we want criminals to become useful members of society when they get out of jail, we must educate them while they are still in prison.

Body →
Education is the key to a prisoner's reform. To create a successful education program, we must enact four measures. First, we must separate nonviolent prisoners or those violent prisoners who wish to change from violent repeat criminals. Then, for prisoners who want to reform, we need to offer a basic skills program because illiteracy is an obstacle for many prisoners. Without knowing how to read, write, and work with numbers, prisoners can't participate in today's job market and end up trapped in a life of crime. For this same reason, up-to-date job training is also essential. In addition to these opportunities, prisoners should have psychological counseling and religious or moral instruction. Because many prisoners have a history of failure and low opinions of themselves, they need to be encouraged to have confidence in their abilities. Prisoners who have job skills and good self-esteem can overcome their depression and feel optimistic about their chance to succeed. Therefore, they will have a higher chance of success in the world outside of prison.

Conclusion →
Prisoners can become better future citizens, but we must educate them while they are still in prison to make their reform a success. By instructing and encouraging those prisoners who are nonviolent or who wish to change, we will not only improve their lives, we will ensure the safety of our society.

1. How do the ideas in the introduction proceed: from general to specific ideas? from specific to general ideas?

2. What is the purpose of the body paragraph?

3. Why do we need a conclusion?

2. The Introduction and the Thesis Statement

The **introduction** of an essay proceeds from general to specific ideas. The last sentence in the introduction, the **thesis statement**, is the most specific idea in the introduction. The thesis statement must communicate a clear idea or opinion; it can never be a statement of fact.

Working with a partner, look back at the introduction of the essay "Education and Criminals." In your notebook, draw a diagram like the one below and copy sentences from the introduction. Put them into three categories: General Ideas, More Specific Ideas, and Most Specific Idea.

General Ideas
(The first sentence(s) of the introduction)
We don't know the exact subject of the essay.
"No man is an island," wrote the English poet John Donne.

More Specific Ideas
(Several more sentences)
The subject becomes clearer.

Most Specific Idea
(The thesis statement)
We know the
author's opinion.

3. The Body

The **body** of an essay gives **support** for the opinion or idea in the thesis statement. Support can include facts, reasons, statistics, explanations, examples, comparisons and contrasts, and recommendations.

Write the four recommendations that the writer makes in the body of the essay "Education and Criminals."

1. We should separate hardened criminals from the others.

2. _____

3. _____

4. _____

4. The Conclusion

A **conclusion** is necessary because it brings an essay to a close. The conclusion refers to ideas in the introduction and the thesis statement. It should not bring up new unrelated ideas. It is best to use different words in the conclusion from those in the introduction to avoid repetition.

Compare the introduction and the conclusion below from the essay, "Education and Criminals"(page 30) and answer the questions below. Write your answers in your notebook.

INTRODUCTION	CONCLUSION
"No man is an island," wrote the English poet John Donne. We are not alone in this world, and what we do has an effect on others. In fact, what we do for prisoners will affect our lives as well as theirs. If we want criminals to become useful members of society when they get out of jail, we must educate them while they are still in prison.	Prisoners can become better future citizens, but we must educate them while they are still in prison to make their reform a success. By instructing and encouraging those prisoners who are nonviolent or who wish to change, we will not only improve their lives, we will ensure the safety of our society.

1. Which idea in the conclusion is the same as the thesis statement?

2. Which part of the conclusion refers to other ideas in the introduction?

5. Practice with Introductions, Thesis Statements, Body Support, and Conclusions

ORGANIZING AN INTRODUCTION

Working with a partner, put these sentences into a logical order to make an essay introduction arguing against education for prisoners. Then circle the sentence that should go last: the thesis statement.

_____   This punishment usually takes the from of a prison sentence.

__1__   We are all members of society.

_____   It would be unreasonable to burden society with the added expense of providing prisoners with a free education.

_____   When we do something that harms society, we have to be punished.

_____   However, it is very expensive to house and feed prisoners.

EVALUATING THESIS STATEMENTS

Decide if the following are good thesis statements. For each one, write "F" for fact, "I" for an inadequate thesis statement, or "T" for a good thesis statement. Discuss your answers with a partner.

___F___ 1. In the past ten years, the crime rate in the United States has gone down, but the prison population has increased.
This is a fact, not an opinion.

___I___ 2. Long prison sentences are important.
This opinion is vague (not clear).

___I___ 3. Now I am going to tell you about criminals and prisons.
This thesis does not give an idea, only an announcement.

___T___ 4. Harsh punishments for criminals will discourage people from turning to a life of crime.
This thesis clearly shows the writer's opinion.

_____ 5. A long prison sentence gives criminals time to think about what they have done.

_____ 6. In 2000, American taxpayers spent approximately $23,000 a year to keep an inmate in prison.

_____ 7. I have always been afraid of criminals. I will tell you why.

_____ 8. Taking young prisoners far away from society and exposing them to harsh conditions in Alaska will help build their characters.

SUPPORTING A THESIS STATEMENT

Look at the thesis statement and the possible support for it below. Working with a partner, put a check (✓) next to the facts and explanations that would be good support in a body paragraph for the thesis statement. Discuss your decisions with your partner.

Thesis Statement

It would be unreasonable to burden society with the added expense of providing prisoners with a free education.

Possible Support

_____ 1. Prisoners hurt society. We need to condemn them to isolation. We should make it hard for visitors to see prisoners by building prisons far away from communities.

_____ 2. Prisoners without skills leave jail with skills.

_____ 3. Prisons cost enough as it is without adding education programs. It is unfair to spend more money on prisons than on public schools.

_____ 4. It is unfair to give criminals an education that many poor people can't afford. This is a luxury that prisoners don't deserve.

_____ 5. More than half of state prison inmates in 1991 had not completed high school before they went to prison; a third were unemployed.

_____ 6. Prisons should not have schools because schools make prison seem like a reward, not a punishment.

CHOOSING THE BEST CONCLUSION

Decide which of these two conclusions would be appropriate for a possible essay called "Prison Should Be a Punishment." Explain your choice in one sentence in your notebook. Compare your answer with a partner's.

Conclusion A

A prison is not a country club. It is a place where prisoners go to be punished for their crimes. Because inmates owe a debt to society, society should not be expected to pay for their education. It would be unfair to charge poor people so much money for higher education and then give free education to criminals.

Conclusion B

If we make prison life attractive, we will never be able to control crime. The crime rate has been falling, but it is still higher in the United States than in most developed countries. I have to worry about crime all the time, and there seems to be danger everywhere. What are we waiting for?

6. Organizing Your Essay

Study this block diagram of a three-paragraph essay to help you organize your essay. In your notebook, draw your own diagram and write your notes in each of its sections.

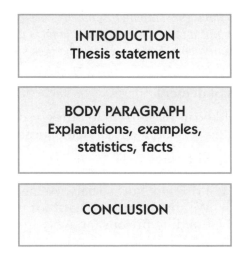

INTRODUCTION
Thesis statement

BODY PARAGRAPH
Explanations, examples, statistics, facts

CONCLUSION

*Write a **first draft** of your essay. Remember to write in complete sentences and try to use some of the vocabulary and structures that you have practiced in this unit.*

C. Revising the First Draft

When you have finished writing your first draft, read it to a partner.

CHECKLIST FOR REVISING THE FIRST DRAFT

When you listen to your partner's essay and when you discuss your own, keep these questions in mind:

1. **Does the introduction give general ideas before specific ones?**

2. **What is the thesis statement? Is it clear?**

3. **What types of support has the writer used in the body paragraph: explanations, facts, statistics, comparisons/contrasts, examples, recommendations? Is there enough support?**

4. **What does the conclusion say? Does it refer back to the main idea in the thesis statement?**

After discussing your essay with a partner, you may want to reorganize what you have written.

*Now write a **second draft** that includes all additions and changes.*

D. Editing the Second Draft

After you have written a second draft, proofread your work for any errors and correct them. These guidelines and exercises should help.

1. Active and Passive Voice

In the **active voice**, the subject of a sentence does the action and is called the **agent.** In the **passive voice**, the subject receives but does not do the action. We use the passive voice when we want to shift the focus from the agent to the object.

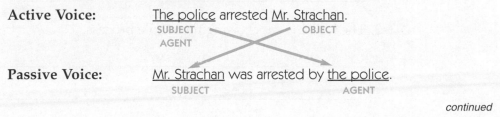

Active Voice: The police arrested Mr. Strachan.
          SUBJECT   OBJECT
          AGENT

Passive Voice: Mr. Strachan was arrested by the police.
          SUBJECT   AGENT

continued

Active Voice

subject [agent] + verb (+ object)

The police arrested Mr. Strachan.

Passive Voice

subject + *be* + past participle (+ *by* + agent)

Mr. Strachan was arrested (by the police).

Active Voice	Passive Voice
The police **arrest** Mr. Strachan.	Mr. Strachan **is arrested** by the police.
are arresting	**is being arrested**
have arrested	**has been arrested**
arrested	**was arrested**
had arrested	**had been arrested**
will arrest	**will be arrested**

In many passive sentences, the agent is not mentioned because it is obvious, unimportant, or unknown.

The Constitution **is recognized** as the supreme law of the United States **(by Americans).**

Change the following sentences from the active voice to the passive voice. Then compare your answers with a partner's.

1. At the beginning of a trial, the defense and prosecuting attorneys interview the potential jurors.

   <u>At the beginning of a trial, the potential jurors are</u>

   <u>interviewed by the defense and prosecuting attorneys.</u>

2. Both lawyers questioned the defendant.

   _____

   _____

3. The judge is supervising the whole process.

   _____

   _____

4. During a trial, all of the witnesses will confront the defendant.

   _____

   _____

5. The jury has heard all of the testimony.

_____

_____

6. By the end of the day, the jury had reached a verdict.

_____

_____

Working with a partner, complete this paragraph about two different philosophies of punishment. Put the sentences in the correct voice: active or passive. Use the verbs in parentheses. Compare your answers with a partner's.

In his essay, "Two Concepts of Rules," political philosopher John Rawls

<u>points out</u> *(point out)* two views of punishment. The first
1

<u>is called</u> *(call)* the retributive view. In this view, the severity of the
2

crime _____ *(determine)* the severity of the punishment. For
3

instance, if the offender takes the life of his victim on purpose, the

retributivists recommend taking the offender's own life as well. If he

accidentally _____ *(kill)* his victim, a lesser punishment
4

_____ *(recommend)*. The retributive view _____
5   6

(understand) best through these words from the Bible: "An eye for an eye, a

tooth for a tooth." Payment for a crime, or retribution, _____
7

(expect) at all times.

The other view _____ *(call)* the utilitarian view, which does not
8

believe that punishment is always necessary. A criminal _____
9

(not / punish) simply because he _____ *(commit)* a crime in the
10

past. Punishment _____ *(recommend)* only if it serves a useful
11

purpose for society. If the criminal has already been reformed and

rehabilitated, punishment _____ *(think)* to be unnecessary.
12

2. Transitive and Intransitive Verbs

Transitive Verbs
Most verbs are **transitive verbs**, which can be used in both the active voice and the passive voice.

to arrest	to be arrested
ACTIVE	PASSIVE

Intransitive Verbs
Some verbs can be used only in the active voice. They are called **intransitive verbs**. They are verbs of being or movement such as *be, become, depend (on), disappear, exist, go (up/down), grow (up), increase, occur, remain, rise, seem,* and *vanish*.

Incorrect	Correct
~~to be occurred~~	to occur
~~to have been occurred~~	to have occurred
~~it is occurred~~	it occurs
~~it was occurred~~	it occurred
~~it has been occurred~~	it has occurred
~~it had been occurred~~	it had occurred
~~it will be occurred~~	it will occur

Read this paragraph about the U.S. correctional system. Put a check (✓) above the verb phrases that are in the correct active or passive voice. Change the phrases that are incorrect. There are five errors.

It seems that the United States is hard on crime. The crime rate

✓
has gone down in the United States while the prison population
1

has been risen. Since 1980, the number of people in state and federal
2

prisons has more than tripled. In addition, the number of people on
3

probation and parole has been grown dramatically in the same period.
4

Altogether, more than 5.3 million people now are remained under some
5

kind of police supervision in the United States.

Because of this, a problem of overcrowding in American prisons

is now existed. The United States has become the country with the most
6   7

people behind bars, with Russia closely following. It must also be considered that high prison population rates have made prison construction a billion-dollar industry. It <u>is occurred</u>[8] to some experts that all this expense may be a waste of money for society. Perhaps the United States depends too much on physical confinement to reduce crime. Is there no other way to stop it?

E. Preparing the Final Draft

Reread your second draft and correct any errors you find. Put a check (✓) in each space as you edit for these points. Then write your corrected final version.

CHECKLIST FOR EDITING THE SECOND DRAFT

_____ active and passive voice
_____ transitive and intransitive verbs

Additional Writing Opportunities

Write about one of the following topics.

1. After reading this update of the Leroy Strachan case, write a letter to the judge. Explain why you agree or disagree with the judge's decision.

UPDATE

Leroy Strachan pleaded guilty to a single count of manslaughter (unintentional killing) in the shooting death of Officer Milledge. The judge of Dade Circuit Court, Miami, Florida, sentenced Leroy Strachan to seven years of supervised probation and 2,000 hours of community service. Strachan returned to New York to live.

---

2. Are you able to forgive people who have been cruel to you? Have you ever had to ask someone to forgive you? Do you believe that we should forget the bad things that happen to us? Write an essay about the idea "forgive and forget." Is this a good way to live?

3. The retributivists believe that punishment for a crime is always necessary. The utilitarians, on the other hand, believe that punishment is only necessary if it benefits society. Which approach do you think is better? Explain why.

4. Many people in the United States favor the death penalty. Do you believe in capital punishment? Why or why not? Express your opinion in a letter to the editor of your local newspaper.

3 MEN AND WOMEN: NOTHING BUT THE FACTS

Gender Poll

	Your Answer	Total
1 In today's world, which has more advantages?		
a. Being a man	____	____
b. Being a woman	____	____
c. It doesn't matter	____	____
2 Do most women you know consider men...		
a. Superior to women?	____	____
b. Inferior to women?	____	____
c. Their equals?	____	____
3 Do most men you know consider women...		
a. Superior to men?	____	____
b. Inferior to men?	____	____
c. Their equals?	____	____
4 How do you want to divide the housework in your marriage?		
a. Fifty percent for each partner	____	____
b. More housework for the husband	____	____
c. More housework for the wife	____	____

WRITING ABOUT GRAPHS AND STATISTICS

In this unit you will practice:

- understanding graphs and statistics
- comparing and contrasting data
- using the language of statistics

Editing focus:

- contrasting verb tenses: the present perfect, simple past, and simple present
- subject-verb agreement

I Fluency Practice: A Poll

Look at the poll above. Answer the questions by putting a check (✓) in the left column on the rows that correspond to your opinion. Share your answers with a partner. Then write the total number of responses from your classmates for each question in the column on the right.

Reading for Writing

This poll from *The New York Times* shows American teenagers' opinions about gender.

Teenagers and Sex Roles

	ALL	GIRLS	BOYS
In today's society, there are more advantages in:			
Being a man	35%	37%	32%
Being a woman	7	8	6
It's the same	55	52	59
Do most girls you know think of boys as:			
Equals	50%	57%	41%
Better than themselves	49	42	56
Do most boys you know think of girls as:			
Equals	36%	34%	39%
Lesser than themselves	61	63	59
How likely is it that you will get married?			
Very likely	63%	65%	62%
Somewhat likely	32	29	34
Not at all likely	4	6	3
How likely is it that you will have children?			
Very likely	55%	57%	53%
Somewhat likely	38	35	41
Not at all likely	6	7	4
Could you have a happy life or would you feel you missed part of what you need to be happy if:			
You don't get married?			
Missed	32%	26%	38%
Still happy	67	73	61
You don't have children?			
Missed	48%	49%	47%
Still happy	51	50	52
You get divorced?			
Missed	30%	22%	37%
Still happy	68	77	60

GIRLS
When you get married, do you expect to . . .

Stay at home 7%
Work 86%

BOYS
When you get married, do you expect your wife to . . .

Stay at home 19%
Work 58%

Based on nationwide telephone interviews with 1,055 teenagers aged 13 to 17 conducted May 26–June 1. "Don't know" answers are excluded.

Source: copyright © 1994 by The New York Times Co.
Reprinted by permission.

A. General Understanding

1. What Do the Statistics Say?

Read these statements about the poll on the previous page and mark them true (T) or false (F). Compare your answers with a partner's.

_____ 1. In this poll, the boys and girls interviewed were 13 to 20 years old.

_____ 2. The boys and girls don't feel the same way about divorce.

_____ 3. The boys who were interviewed said that most boys they know think boys and girls are equals.

_____ 4. The girls who were interviewed said that most girls they know think boys and girls are equals.

_____ 5. Most of the boys and girls expect to get married.

_____ 6. The girls think that having children is more important than getting married.

2. What Proof Do You Have?

Provide proof for statements about the poll on the previous page. First study the connectors, statement, and proof in the box below. Then write at least one sentence to prove each of the statements on the next page. Use connectors and statistics in your sentences. When you have finished, read your sentences to a partner.

CONNECTORS

Connectors Showing Similarity	Connectors Showing Difference
and	but, however
like	while, although
both	unlike

Statement
Boys and girls don't feel the same way about divorce.

Proof
Like most boys, most girls expect to get married. **However**, they have different views about divorce.

Divorce would make only 22 percent of girls unhappy, **but / while / although** it would make 37 percent of boys unhappy.

1. Most of the boys and girls see no advantage to being a boy instead of a girl.

_____

_____

2. The boys and girls do not agree on whether wives should work after marriage.

_____

_____

3. Most of the boys and girls expect to have children.

_____

_____

4. Most of the girls say that boys they know do not think boys and girls are equals.

_____

_____

5. Most of the girls say they would still be happy if they got divorced. Only some girls would not be happy if they got divorced.

_____

_____

3. What Conclusions Can You Reach?

Read these statements. Write "Yes" if the statistics from the poll on page 42 support these conclusions or "No" if they do not.

_____ 1. Girls have a more negative opinion of divorce than boys have.

_____ 2. Some girls may choose to have children without being married.

_____ 3. Boys today are more traditional than boys were 30 years ago.

_____ 4. Boys don't want to get married.

_____ 5. Most girls expect to work after they get married.

_____ 6. Boys and girls in this survey have opposing views about gender equality.

4. Converting Statistics from a Paragraph to a Graph

Read this paragraph about women and men in the U.S. workplace. Then convert the statistics into three bar charts. Use the example to help you. When you have finished, compare your graphs with a partner's.

Although American women made progress in the workplace toward the end of the 20th century, they still did not enjoy equal status with men in 1999. For instance, U.S. government statistics for that year showed that women made up 76.3 percent of the administrative and clerical positions (for example, secretaries and typists) but only 46.7 percent of the top executive and managerial positions. Although 33 percent of lawyers were women, only 27.5 percent of judges were women. Men still made more money and had more job status than women at the end of the 20th century.

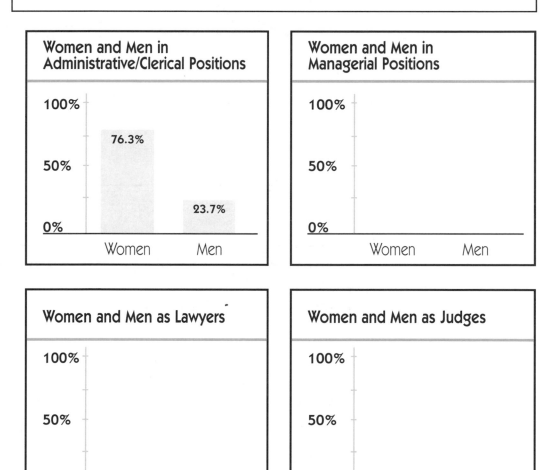

B. Working with Language

The Gender Gap

Study the graph and the vocabulary below. Then complete the paragraphs on the next page with the appropriate words. Some words may be used more than once. Be sure to put verbs in the simple past or present perfect tense. When you have finished, compare your answers with a partner's.

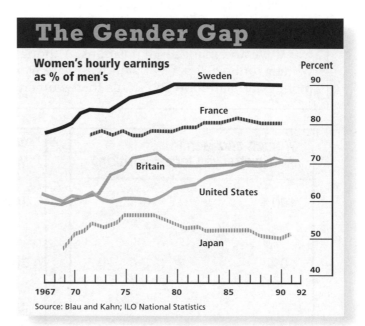

Adjectives	Nouns	Noun Phrase
gradual slight steady sharp steep	rise increase growth fall decrease decline	a gradual rise
Verbs	**Adverbs**	**Verb Phrase**
to rise to go up to increase to grow to fall to go down to decrease to decline	slightly (a little) gradually (slowly) steadily (without changing) sharply (quickly) steeply	to rise slightly

The Gender Gap in Wages

When women and men are paid unequal wages for the same job, we call this a "gender wage gap." Since 1967 women's wages _have risen_ in relation to men's wages, but in most countries women have not achieved complete equality in the workplace. The graph "The Gender Gap" shows this inequality by comparing statistics between the United States, Japan, and three European countries near the end of the 20th century.

Swedish women were paid wages most equal to men's in 1992. Women's wages in Sweden rose _____ from 1967 to 1980 to reach about 90 percent of men's wages. The figure then remained about the same until the 1990s. By comparison, the French figure did not _____ as much as the Swedish figure did between 1972 and 1976. French women's wages rose _____ to only 80 percent of men's in 1990. In Britain, there was a _____ _____ in women's wages from 1970 to 1976. The figure leveled off at 10 percentage points below the French figure in 1990. Unlike Sweden and France, the United States saw almost no improvement in the wage gap before 1978, but in 1978 there was a _____ _____ in U.S. wages for women. Yet in 1990 women still received no more than 70 percent of men's wages in the United States. In Japan, women's wages _____ until 1975. After 1978 they _____ steadily until 1990, when they were only 50 percent of men's wages.

The statistics show that the gender wage gap is slowly narrowing in Europe and the United States. Sweden, in particular, gives women wages that are almost equal to men's. More research should be conducted to understand how to solve the gender wage gap.

III ◆ Prewriting Activities

A. Point-of-View Writing

Read each quote and explain the feelings expressed. Read your answers to a partner.

1. "In our company, women should be paid the same as men for the same job."

   How would this manager explain his position?

   _____

   _____

2. "I know a lot of girls who think it is sexist to say that girls belong in the kitchen. They say we boys should help with the cleaning, but I think they're wrong. Cleaning is not a boy's job."

   How would this student explain his viewpoint?

   _____

   _____

3. "I think a career is most important, then children, then marriage."

   How would this student explain her position?

   _____

   _____

B. Open for Discussion

Discuss these quotes in a small group. Then choose one quote. In your notebook, summarize your opinion of it and the opinion of someone who disagreed with you. Write three sentences for each summary.

1. "A woman's place is in the home."
2. "A man or woman who stays at home to raise children doesn't need a college education."
3. "Boys and girls should be encouraged to play with the same toys when they are little."
4. "Fathers need to be as involved in their children's lives as mothers are."

IV ▸ Structured Writing Focus

YOUR TASK

Write a three-paragraph essay on the statistics from the series of tables below. You may write on one, two, or all of the tables.

ALTERNATIVE TASK: Find a different graph on the topic of gender differences and write a three-paragraph essay on it.

Table A — Women's University Degrees
Proportion of Degrees Awarded to Women

	B.A.'s	Ph.D.'s	M.D.'s	Law	M.B.A.'s	Engineering
1960	38.5%	10.5%	5.5%	2.5%	3.6%	0.4%
1970	43.1%	13.3%	8.4%	5.4%	3.6%	0.8%
1980	49.0%	29.7%	23.4%	30.2%	22.4%	9.3%
1996	55.1%	45.4%	40.9%	43.5%	37.6%	16.1%

Source: U.S. National Center for Educational Statistics

Table B — Women's Work and Pay
Percentage of Jobs Held by Women

	1970	1998
Managers and Executives	16.7%	44.4%
College faculty	28.6%	42.3%
Economists	11.4%	46.3%
Psychologists	38.5%	62.1%
Pharmacists	12.0%	44.0%
Architects	3.6%	17.5%

Source: Bureau of Labor Statistics

Table C — Brides, Grooms, and Babies

At First Marriage	Average Bride's Age	Average Groom's Age	Children per 100 Women
1960	20.3	22.8	345
1970	20.8	23.5	248
1980	22	24.7	184
1990	23.9	26.1	208
1998	25	26.7	203

Source: Bureau of the Census and National Center for Health Statistics

A. Starting to Write

Brainstorming

Answer these questions on the table or tables that you have chosen for your writing task. Mark these statements true (T) or false (F). Then compare your answers with a partner who is working on the same table(s).

TABLE A: WOMEN'S UNIVERSITY DEGREES

_____ 1. More women than men graduated with B.A.'s in 1960.

_____ 2. The percentage of male graduates in engineering in 1996 was about the same as it was in 1960.

_____ 3. The percentage of female graduates in medicine and law in 1996 was greater than in business and engineering.

TABLE B: WOMEN'S WORK AND PAY

_____ 1. From 1970 to 1998 the greatest change in the percentage of jobs held by women was in college teaching and architecture.

_____ 2. In 1998 women outnumbered men only as psychologists.

_____ 3. In 1998 women and men were most equally represented in the field of architecture.

TABLE C: BRIDES, GROOMS, AND BABIES

_____ 1. The marrying age of men and women has steadily increased from 1960 to 1998.

_____ 2. From 1960 until 1998, brides were usually older than grooms.

_____ 3. The birth rate declined between 1960 and 1998.

Write answers in your notebook to these questions about the table(s) that you have chosen to help you write your essay.

1. What is interesting about the statistics you chose?

2. Do the statistics show changing roles of men and women or inequality between them?

3. Can you reach any general conclusions from these statistics or by comparing the different tables?

4. For your conclusion: If your tables(s) show gender inequality, how would you recommend solving this inequality?

B. Preparing the First Draft

1. Analyzing Essay Structure

Look back at the essay "The Gender Gap in Wages" on page 47. Working with a partner, and writing in your own words, answer these questions in your notebook.

1. What is the main idea of the introduction?

2. How do the statistics in the body support the main idea?

3. What conclusion is reached from these statistics?

2. Expressions for Writing on Statistics

Study the expressions below. Then write four sentences in your notebook using these expressions to describe the tables on page 49.

COMPARISON/CONTRAST

more than / less than / fewer than
Girls have a **more** positive view of divorce **than** boys do.
Boys have a **less** positive view of divorce **than** girls do.
Fewer boys **than** girls think they are equals.

the same as
The requirements to enter law school are almost **the same as** the requirements to enter graduate school.

(not) as . . . as
Medical students are **(not) as** anxious **as** law students are about their exams.

compared with / as opposed to
Compared with teachers, medical doctors earn a lot of money.
Only 16 percent of engineers, **as opposed to** 41 percent of medical doctors, are women.

different from
Law exams are **different from** business exams.

CAUSE AND CONSEQUENCE

as . . . , more . . .
As more women go to college, **more** women start professional careers.

as . . . , fewer . . .
As more women graduate from college, **fewer** women are stay-at-home moms.

PERCENTAGES AND FRACTIONS

out of
At least four **out of** every ten pharmacists were women three decades later.

3. Organizing Your Essay

Study this block diagram of a three-paragraph essay to plan a first draft of your essay. In your notebook, draw your own diagram and write your notes in each of its sections.

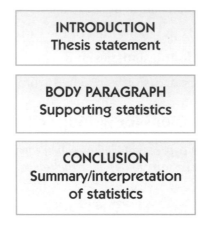

INTRODUCTION
Thesis statement

BODY PARAGRAPH
Supporting statistics

CONCLUSION
Summary/interpretation
of statistics

*Write a **first draft** of your essay. Remember to write in complete sentences and try to use some of the vocabulary and structures that you have practiced in this unit.*

C. Revising the First Draft

When you have finished writing, read your first draft to someone who has chosen at least one different table.

CHECKLIST FOR REVISING THE FIRST DRAFT

When you listen to your partner's essay and when you discuss your own, keep these questions in mind:

1. **Does the introduction first mention the general topic of the table(s) or graph(s) and end with a thesis statement (main idea) about the table(s) or graph(s)?**

2. **Does the body give statistics to support the thesis statement?**

3. **Does the conclusion refer back to the thesis statement and offer possible explanations for the statistics or suggest other areas of research?**

After discussing your essay with a partner, you may want to add, change, or omit some ideas.

*Now write a **second draft** that includes all of your additions and changes.*

D. Editing the Second Draft

After you have written a second draft, proofread your work for any errors and correct them. These guidelines and exercises should help.

1. Contrasting Verb Tenses

Simple Past	**Present Perfect**	**Simple Present**
In 1960 fewer women than men **graduated** from college.	Since 1960 many more women **have graduated** from college.	Today more women than men **graduate** from college.

THE PRESENT PERFECT

The **present perfect** often describes an action that began in the past and continues into the present.

have + past participle
More women **have graduated** since 1960.

Some time expressions showing the need for the present perfect are:

since 1960
for forty **years**
in the past forty **years**

THE SIMPLE PAST

The **simple past** describes an action that happened in the past and is not continuing in the present. Some time expressions showing the need for the simple past are:

in 1960
forty years **ago**
at that time

THE SIMPLE PRESENT

The **simple present** describes an action that happens in the present. Some time expressions showing the need for the simple present are:

today
now
nowadays
at present

Working with a partner, complete the following paragraphs by writing the verb in parentheses in the correct tense: present perfect, simple past, or simple present.

According to U.S. Census Bureau information on annual earnings averages, since 1983 women <u>have made</u> (make) some progress in the
 1
workplace in most professions. The following statistics _____
 2
(provide) data showing that recently more women _____ *(enter)* the
 3
workforce, yet they still make less than men do.

In the past 20 years the percentage of women in professional positions
_____ *(grow)*. For example, 46.8 percent of professional workers
 4
_____ *(be)* women in 1983, while 52 percent of these workers
 5
_____ *(be)* women in 1999. Although women participate more in the
 6
workforce than they _____ *(do)* in the past, they still make less
 7
money than men make. Professional women _____ *(do not earn)* as
 8
much as their male counterparts did in 1999. Their average earnings
_____ *(increase)* only slightly between 1983 and 1999. Women's
 9
earnings _____ *(be)* 72.6 percent of professional men's in 1983 and
 10
increased to only 76.5 percent of men's in 1999. That means that for every
dollar a male professional _____ *(receive)* for his services in 1999, a
 11
woman received just over 75 cents.

Although it is obvious that women _____ *(make)* progress in the
 12
professional workforce since 1983, they are still paid less than men for the
same job. Employers must pay women wages equal to those of men's for
women to have full equality with men in the future.

2. Subject-Verb Agreement

All verbs must agree in number with the subject nouns that they refer to. This includes nouns that show a quantity or percentage.

	Singular Subject		**Third Person Singular Verb**
The	**number**	of male graduates	**has** fallen.
The	**proportion/percentage**	of female graduates	**has** increased.
The	**ratio**	of male to female graduates	**is** changing.

	Plural Subject		**Third Person Plural Verb**
The	**percentages**	of female students	**have** changed.
The	**ratios**	of degrees awarded	**are changing.**

Working with a partner, correct these sentences for subject-verb agreement. Put a check (✓) over the correct sentences. If the subject and verb do not agree, cross out the incorrect verb tense and write the correct one above it.

1. The number of bachelor's degrees awarded to women **has increased**. ✓

2. The percentage of graduate degrees going to women **has** also **changed**.

3. The number of women receiving Ph.D.'s today **are** almost the same as the number of men receiving them.

4. The proportion of women receiving medical degrees **has risen** steadily.

5. In 1996 the ratio of female to male doctors **were** two to three.

6. Nevertheless, the proportion of women receiving medical degrees **is rising** steadily.

E. Preparing the Final Draft

Reread your second draft and correct any errors you find. Put a check (✓) in each space as you edit for these points. Then write your corrected final version.

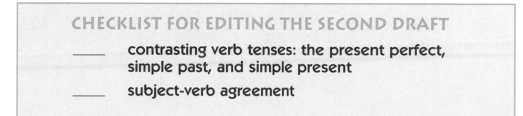

CHECKLIST FOR EDITING THE SECOND DRAFT

_____ contrasting verb tenses: the present perfect, simple past, and simple present

_____ subject-verb agreement

Additional Writing Opportunities

Write about one of the following topics.

1. Find a series of graphs or tables on a subject of your choice. Study the figures and write an essay analyzing the meaning of the graphs.

2. Write an essay explaining your opinion of the saying, "A woman's place is in the home." Do you agree or disagree?

3. Some young men today want to be better fathers to their children than the fathers of previous generations were to their children. What are your feelings on this issue? Write an essay explaining how to be the ideal father.

4. "It would be ridiculous to talk of male and female atmospheres, male or female springs or rains, male and female sunshine. How much more ridiculous is it in relation to mind, to soul, to thought, where there is just as undeniably no such thing as sex, to talk of male and female education and male and female schools."

(Susan B. Anthony and Elizabeth Cady Stanton)

This quote, written almost a century ago, expresses the opinion of two leaders of the American movement for equal rights for women. Today some people still defend single-sex schools. Some women prefer all-female high schools and colleges because women have more opportunities to take on leadership roles and don't have to compete with men. Some men prefer to attend all-male schools because they can concentrate more on studies and less on the opposite sex.

What do you think? Do you prefer coed schools (schools that educate men and women together) or single-sex schools? Explain your answer in a letter to the editor of your school newspaper.

UNIT
4 THE BEST TIME
TO BE ALIVE

WRITING A
FIVE-PARAGRAPH ESSAY

In this unit you will practice:
- explaining reasons
- identifying effective thesis statements
- writing topic sentences
- creating coherent paragraph order
- choosing the best conclusion

Editing focus:
- adjective clauses
- present unreal conditionals

I Fluency Practice: Freewriting

If you could choose another time in history to visit, which time period would you choose? What country would you choose? What would you hope to discover?

Write for ten minutes on any of these questions. Try to express yourself as well as you can. Don't worry about mistakes. Share your writing with a partner.

II ► Reading for Writing

In this abridged and adapted interview from *The New York Times Magazine*, a famous newspaper columnist asks several distinguished people to describe the ideal time to live.

THERE'S NO TIME LIKE THE PAST

Participants:

Russell Baker, columnist for *The New York Times*

Thomas Cahill, author of *How the Irish Saved Civilization*

Ann Douglas, Professor of English, Columbia University

Elaine Pagels, Professor of Religion, Princeton University

Orlando Patterson, Professor of Sociology, Harvard University

Jonathan Spence, Professor of History, Yale University

BAKER: None of us are living in today's world by choice. Maybe, given our choice, we would prefer to be somewhere else. I would bet in most
5 cases not in the future. I suppose some people would say that today is the ideal time. I'm prepared to argue against that, but I'm here to listen to your opinions. Mr. Spence, you would
10 probably like to go back in time?

Hangzhou, China

SPENCE: Absolutely. I would be very interested to live my life in Hangzhou, a beautiful city in China. I know where my villa would be: on the west side of the lake in the hills, looking down on what was then an unpolluted lake, in what was a prosperous[1] rural resort town. It would be around 1540. I
15 would want to have a little bit of money. I wouldn't want too much because the officials from Beijing[2] would take it away from me. The Ming dynasty[3] was one of the most sophisticated and cultured times in all of Chinese history. People read a great deal. It was a magnificent time in painting. The food was wonderful. It was not a slave society. It was a rich time to
20 live.

BAKER: It sounds like a paradise. What about you, Mr. Patterson?

---

1. *prosperous:* wealthy, rich
2. *Beijing:* capital of China
3. *Ming dynasty:* The period in China (1368–1644) when the rulers were all descendants of the Ming family

PATTERSON: I have two choices. . . . My second choice is to have lived in Tokugawa Japan, in the 18th century. I would not have been a Samurai.[4] By then, the Samurai were no longer warriors;[5] they were almost
25 government bureaucrats. I would want to have been a moderately wealthy merchant in the 1730s. I would have liked disobeying the shogun, the military ruler. When the shogun said, "You can no longer wear
30 fancy[6] clothes; you have to wear cotton if you are a merchant," the merchants wore cotton on the outside, but silk on the inside! I would have loved Kabuki dramas.[7] I think people lived longer in Japan than in Europe
35 at that time. And it was very peaceful. My first choice is the 14th century, in a city-state that produced some of the most beautiful art in the world. Can you guess which city-state I have in mind? The town of
40 Ife in Yorubaland, in what is now western Nigeria. I would want to have been a sculptor, one of the people who produced those incredible bronze heads or the terra-cotta work you can now see in the
45 British Museum. Again, the life expectancy —how long people expected to live—was possibly much longer than for a working man in Europe at that time.

Kabuki actor

Ife terracotta head

DOUGLAS: We're all imagining ourselves as
50 having a privileged position in societies in the past. We are very privileged in today's society, so it's natural that we see ourselves that way in the past.

PATTERSON: These sculptors were not very privileged people. They were
55 just comfortable.

DOUGLAS: All I'm saying is that I would not want to be a serf.[8] What matters most to me is to live in an age where things are changing, and where I,

continued

---

4. *Samurai:* members of the military class of Japan (1193–1868)
5. *warriors:* fighters
6. *fancy:* expensive, elaborate
7. *Kabuki dramas:* traditional Japanese theater in which male actors play both men's and women's roles and wear white face makeup.
8. *serf:* During the Middle Ages in Europe (A.D. 500–1300), serfs were poor farmers who worked on their master's estate and could not leave it.

as a woman, could play a part in it. In other words, if I lived in 1789 in France during the French Revolution or in the American colonies in 1779, 60 I might not have been able to play a direct part in those revolutions. So the best time for me would have been in 19th-century New England, in the 1830s, '40s and '50s, at the time of the abolitionist movement against slavery. It was a time when women became professional authors in this country. They could actually make a living not just as schoolteachers but 65 also as writers. Some of the women writers at this time were the main economic support of their families. I can't really see myself back much before that period.

BAKER: I wonder if I could change the focus to the idea of progress. Do we all believe in progress?

70 **CAHILL:** I would like to speak for progress. We have seen the end of the bloodiest of all the centuries to be sure, but I think people are aware of the necessity for peace. It is not a universal awareness, by any means, but it is there.

PAGELS: Can I say something about progress? First of all, I think of 75 medical progress. With the best medical care in the year A.D. 160, the emperor of Rome and his wife had 13 children and 9 of them died before they grew up. Mozart's wife in Austria in the 18th century had 9 children and I believe that 7 of them died. And that was just taken for granted in all countries in the past. There has also been technological progress. Today, 80 technology has changed so much, including the nature of work for millions of people in all parts of the world. Most important is that more and more people are forced by global communications to deal with other cultures. It's much harder to be closed off from the rest of the world, unaware of people who are different from you. There's a different sense of human 85 society and humankind in today's world.

A. General Understanding

Match the topics discussed in the interview with the countries that they describe. Put a check (✓) in the appropriate column. Some topics may describe more than one country. Share your answers with a partner.

Topics	China 1540s	Japan 1730s	Nigeria 1300s	U.S.A. 1800s
1. The environment				
2. The arts				
3. Life expectancy				
4. Political activism				
5. Wealth				
6. Peace				

Answer these questions in your own words in your notebook. You may have to infer the meaning, that is, guess what the speaker suggests but does not say openly. Share your answers with a partner.

1. Russell Baker does not believe that the present is the best time to live. What reasons might he give to explain his opinion?

2. When Jonathan Spence describes the Ming dynasty as "a rich time to live," what does he mean?

3. What attracts Orlando Patterson to the lifestyle of merchants in Tokugawa Japan?

4. Why did Orlando Patterson choose 14th-century Ife as his ideal time to live?

5. If Ann Douglas were a man, would she still choose 19th-century America as the best time to live? Why or why not?

6. Some people say that life was better in the past. Would Elaine Pagels agree or disagree? What evidence does she give to support her view?

B. Working with Language

Read this story about 1920s New York. Replace the words beneath the blanks with their synonyms from the bolded words below.

bureaucrats	**determined**	**economic**	**incredible**
privileged	**prosperous**	**sophisticated**	**unpolluted**

New York City in the 1920s

When my great-aunt was a young girl in the 1920s, New York City was very different from the way it is today. The air was __unpolluted__ and
1) clean
because there was so little crime, people didn't even lock their doors! Entertainment was more simple and not as _____ as it is today:
2) complex
No one had TV, children played freely in the streets and parks, and silent movies were a Saturday treat.

In the 1920s, the successful stock market made the city _____.
3) wealthy
Although there were jobs for everyone, only some people were

_____ enough to go to college. Many people took civil service
4) fortunate
exams and worked for the city as laborers or as _____. It was
5) government workers
not very easy for women to get an education or a good job. My great-aunt

was one of many _____ women who became secretaries. The
6) strong-willed
law firm where she worked for almost 50 years made her very comfortable

in _____ terms. But in those days it was hard for a working
7) financial
woman to get married and have a family. Today women can have it all: a

family and a career. How _____ our life would seem to my
8) unbelievable
great-aunt!

III Prewriting Activities

A. Point-of-View Writing

Write a letter to a great-grandparent or another relative who lived in the past. Explain how life today is different from the way it was before. Use the style below to help you.

Dear _____,

_____

_____

_____

_____

_____

_____

_____

Love,

_____

B. Science Fiction

Read these plot descriptions of science fiction novels and films that warn us about the future. Write one sentence that explains the warning in each. If you have seen one of the films, explain the plot and the main idea in more detail in your notebook.

1. *Fahrenheit 451*
(a novel by Ray Bradbury, U.S.A., and a film by François Truffaut, France)

This story takes place in a world where firemen are responsible for setting fires, not putting them out. The firemen burn books because the government thinks books are dangerous. In this society, people must watch mindless TV programs all the time. Everyone thinks the same thoughts except for the "outlaws" who live in the woods. These outlaws prevent the ideas from the books from being lost by memorizing them and teaching them to young people.

_____

_____

2. *Soylent Green*
(a film by Richard Fleischer, U.S.A.)

In this film, New York City is completely polluted in 2022. It is always 90°F and there is no sunlight—nothing but darkness and dirty air. There is no oil to make electricity, and three quarters of the population is homeless. The soil is so polluted that farming is impossible. Only the rich can afford to eat lettuce or beef, while most people have to eat "soylent" crackers supposedly made from soybeans.

_____

_____

3. *Gattaca*
(a film by Andrew Niccol, U.S.A.)

In this future society, people no longer have children by natural means. Instead, they go to scientists who create babies with perfectly manipulated genes. Everywhere people go they must give blood samples so that their DNA can be inspected. The society judges people by their DNA, which alone determines whether the person is smart or healthy enough to get a good job. If a person's DNA is not "good," he or she has no hope to succeed. One man with "bad" DNA tries to prove his intelligence.

_____

_____

C. Open for Discussion

Discuss these questions in a small group. Then choose one question and summarize the group's discussion on it in your notebook.

1. Was life in the past better or worse than it is today? How?

2. Do you like science fiction stories? Tell the plot of a science fiction story that you have read or a movie that you have seen. What was the main idea and how did you react to it?

3. Some people see the future as a utopia where everything will be wonderful. Others think the future will be a dystopia—a terrible time and place to live. What do you think the future will be?

4. Do you think it is important for society to treasure art and music? How can it do this?

5. Describe the best time to be alive—past, present, or future—and where.

IV Structured Writing Focus

Write a five-paragraph essay describing the best time or the worst time (past, present, or future) to be alive and why.

ALTERNATIVE TASK: Write a five-paragraph essay explaining the reasons why you think we should study the past. Does the past teach us lessons for the future?

A. Starting to Write

Brainstorming

To decide which time period you want to write about, write all of your ideas about the past, the present, and the future in your notebook. Then choose the time with the most interesting notes for your first draft. Consider these questions to help you write.

FOR THE MAIN TASK

The Past
What time in the past is the most interesting for you? What characteristics of a past society make it attractive or unattractive to you: art? gold? conquests? castles? beauty? peace?

The Present
If you think that the present is the best time to live, is it because you love the place where you live? What characteristics of the present make it positive or negative for you?

The Future
Will the future be better or worse than the present? What will it bring us? What are you looking forward to?

FOR THE ALTERNATIVE TASK

What great crimes have occurred in the past centuries? Has civilization learned from any of these past crimes, so that they have not been repeated? Or has society still not learned from history? What facts can you give to support your opinion?

What can we learn by studying the arts, sciences, languages, customs, beliefs, or religions of past societies?

B. Preparing the First Draft

1. Analyzing Essay Structure

Read this student's first draft and identify the parts of the essay: introduction, body paragraphs 1, 2, and 3, and conclusion. When you have finished, answer the questions on the next page in your notebook and compare your answers with a partner's.

STUDENT ESSAY FIRST DRAFT

Living in the Present

a. _____

I have been interested in history ever since I was in junior high school. Sometimes I have wondered about living in another time. What would my life have been like? But if someone asked me today when I would like to live, I would say the present. Peace, a chance for women, and the love of my family and friends are the reasons why I would choose to live my life at the present time.

b. _____

The present is important to me as a woman because it is only today that women can show their true contributions to society. In the past, it wasn't easy for women because they couldn't study or work. They had to stay home and take care of their husbands and children. I don't want to say that family isn't important. On the contrary, family is essential to my life, but the chance to work and study is also valuable. Today, many women play an important role in the professional world, something they could not have done in the past.

c. _____

Although it is not perfect and we still have problems, our time is more peaceful than other times in the past. In fact, I think people in the past would feel that our time is very close to the ideal because we have hope for peace in the future.

d. _____

The third reason why I prefer the present is more personal. I could never bear to be separated from my family and friends. My family is the best that anyone could have, and I can't imagine living without them. My friends are also a key to my happiness, and I would not want to be lost in the past with an empty heart. I know that in any time I lived I would look for close friends, but I am convinced I would never find better ones than those I already have.

e. _____

For me the present is the best time because I can live in peace, develop as a woman, and enjoy the people I care about.

1. Why was the writer so interested in the past? What details or stories could the writer add to get the reader's attention?

2. Circle the thesis statement. Could it be clearer?

3. Do the body paragraphs follow the order of the ideas in the thesis statement?

4. What explanation could be added to give more support for the body paragraph on peace?

5. Is the conclusion long enough? What could the writer add to the conclusion to develop it more?

6. Do you have any other comments?

Now read this second draft of the student essay. Answer the questions that follow. Then compare your answers with those of your classmates and your teacher.

STUDENT ESSAY SECOND DRAFT

Living in the Present

I have been interested in history ever since I was in junior high school. Sometimes I have daydreamed about the past and the life I could have had. I still love to read about ancient civilizations, like ancient Egypt, but if I had to choose when I would like to live, I would never choose the past. The present is the best time for me as a woman because living in a world at peace, being able to develop my mind and talents, and enjoying the love of my family and friends are the most important things in my life.

Our time is more peaceful than most other times in the past. In fact, I think past generations would look at our lives today, in developed countries, and think that they are close to the ideal. Although there are still conflicts in some parts of the world, we have lived for more than 60 years without world war. We have not suffered the tragedies of war as past generations did. In addition, today we are more concerned about what is happening in the world. Before and even after World War II, people tended to think only about their own lives and countries. Now that we care more about international problems, we are making the world more peaceful.

The present is important to me as a woman because I can develop my mind and talents. It is only now that women can begin to show their full contribution to the world. In the past, women's lives were not easy because they couldn't study or work outside of the home. They had to take care of their husbands and children. I don't want to say that family isn't important. On the contrary, family is essential to my life, but the chance to work and study is also valuable. Today, many women play an important role in the professional world, something that they couldn't have done in the past.

continued

The third reason why I prefer the present is even more personal: I could never bear to be separated from my family and friends. My family is the best that anyone could have, and I can't imagine living without them. My friends are also essential to my happiness, and I wouldn't want to be lost in the past with an empty heart. I know that in any time I lived I would look for close friends, but I'm convinced I would never find better ones than those that I already have.

I hope that I can use these years of peace, this chance to develop independently as a woman, and the support of the people I love to create a happy and productive future. Studying history reminds us that many people in the past tried to make the world a better place. I hope to do the same and to live my life to the fullest today and tomorrow.

1. Was the introduction more interesting in the second draft?

2. Do the body paragraphs now follow the order of ideas in the thesis statement?

3. How does the body paragraph on peace give more support in the second draft?

4. Is the new conclusion more meaningful?

5. Do you have any other comments?

2. The Thesis Statement: Creating Unity

The thesis statement of an essay creates **unity**—one overarching idea. A good thesis statement is supported by the other ideas, explanations, and examples in the introduction, body paragraph(s), and conclusion.

Read each sentence below. If it would make a good thesis statement for a five-paragraph essay, write "Yes." If it would not, write "No" and explain your answer.

<u>No</u> 1. The present is the best time for me to live, although perhaps this is not true for everyone.

Explanation: _opinion not clear; no reasons are given_

<u>No</u> 2. We cannot know what the future will bring.

Explanation: _gives a fact, not an opinion_

_____ 3. In the future, the development of technology, the spread of democracy, and the discoveries of medicine will change the world we live in and the way we think.

Explanation: _____

68   Unit 4

_____ 4. The future will be a utopia beyond our imagination.

   Explanation: _____

_____ 5. With its small communities and close relationships, life in the past
         was more human: less stressful, less cruel, and more compatible
         with nature.

   Explanation: _____

_____ 6. I'd like to tell you about the time that would be perfect for me to
         live in.

   Explanation: _____

_____ 7. Despite the efforts of our research, scholarship, and imagination,
         we can never completely recapture the past.

   Explanation: _____

3. Topic Sentences: Connecting the Body to the Thesis

The topic sentence is usually the first sentence of each body paragraph.
It restates one of the ideas or reasons from the thesis statement. The rest
of the paragraph describes the idea found in the topic sentence. Topic
sentences connect the ideas in the body paragraphs to the thesis statement.

_Study the thesis statement and topic sentences below from the second draft of the
studenl essay, "Living in the Present." Then check your answers for Exercise 2, The
Thesis Statement: Creating Unity. In your notebook, write three topic sentences for
one of the good thesis statements. Compare your topic sentences with a partner and
with the class._

Thesis Statement

The present is the best time for me as a woman because living in a **world at
peace,** being able to **develop my mind and talents,** and enjoying the **love
of my family and friends** are the most important things in my life.

Body ¶1 Topic Sentence	Body ¶2 Topic Sentence	Body ¶3 Topic Sentence
Our time is more peaceful than most other times in the past.	The present is important to me as a woman because I can develop my mind and talents.	The third reason why I prefer the present is even more personal: I could never bear to be separated from my family and friends.

4. Paragraph Order: Creating Coherence

Coherence means that the ideas within and between paragraphs are logically organized. Coherence is created in part through a logical paragraph order. There are many types of logical paragraph order, as shown in the examples below.

Study these examples of logical paragraph order. Then in your notebook, write the order the student uses for the essay on pages 67–68.

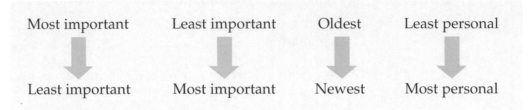

Most important	Least important	Oldest	Least personal
↓	↓	↓	↓
Least important	Most important	Newest	Most personal

5. Choosing the Best Conclusion

Read the thesis statement and the main ideas for body paragraphs that would follow it. Put a check (✓) next to the best conclusion. Discuss your answer with a partner.

Thesis Statement

The best time for me to live would be the past because I would be able to live a simple life, I could escape from modern times and into the old village life, and I could see my country when its traditions were intact.

Body Paragraph	Main Ideas
¶1	Time passed more slowly and we lived closer to nature.
¶2	People lived in a close-knit community, and family and village were in harmony.
¶3	My country followed its own customs and traditions.

_____ Conclusion A

I would love a life of working on the land with my friends and family around me. I am better suited to the friendly village life of the past than to the hectic and impersonal life of today. But the best part about going back to the past would be seeing my country's old customs and traditions. The past is always with us. We must try to keep the past generations alive in our hearts by upholding their traditions. This is the only way to make modern life a blessing and not a terrible loss of our past memories.

_____ **Conclusion B**

   I would like to go back to the past because modern life is too fast-paced for me. I am lonely and lost in big cities, and I don't enjoy studying all day in a closed room. Getting an education from books is dry and meaningless to me; it is not as good as learning from life. I love the past because people had more contact with nature and one another. The past is the time that I was meant to live in.

6. Organizing Your Essay

Study this block diagram of a five-paragraph essay to plan a first draft of your essay. In your notebook, draw your own diagram and write your notes in each of its sections.

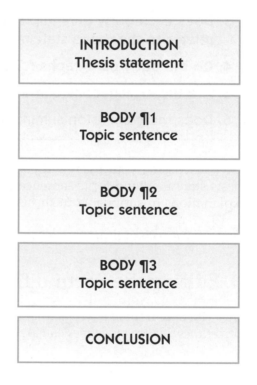

*Write a **first draft** of your essay. Remember to write in complete sentences and try to use some of the vocabulary and structures that you have practiced in this unit.*

C. Revising the First Draft

When you have finished writing your first draft, read it to a partner.

CHECKLIST FOR REVISING THE FIRST DRAFT

When you listen to your partner's essay and when you discuss your own, keep these questions in mind:

1. Does the introduction begin with general ideas and end with a specific thesis statement?

2. Does your thesis statement give one central idea or opinion with reasons to support it?

3. Does each body paragraph begin with a topic sentence that relates to the thesis statement?

4. Do the body paragraphs follow in a logical order?

5. Are the explanations convincing in each body paragraph?

6. Does the conclusion summarize the main points of the essay?

After discussing your essay with a partner, you may want to change your thesis statement and topic sentences. You might also want to add more explanations to support your thesis.

*Now write a **second draft** that includes all of your additions and changes.*

D. Editing the Second Draft

After you have written a second draft, proofread your work for any errors and correct them. These guidelines and exercises should help.

1. Adjective Clauses

COMBINING SENTENCES WITH ADJECTIVE CLAUSES

Short sentences can be combined into longer, complex sentences by using **adjective clauses**. An adjective clause immediately follows the noun that it defines.

The Shogun was a military leader. The Shogun ruled feudal Japan.

The Shogun was a military <u>leader</u> **who ruled feudal Japan.**

NOUN   ADJECTIVE CLAUSE

FORMING ADJECTIVE CLAUSES WITH WHO, THAT, WHICH, WHERE, OR WHEN*

people + *who* or *that*
Samurai warriors were <u>men</u> **who protected Japanese lords.**

Samurai warriors were <u>men</u> **that protected Japanese lords.**

things + *that* or *which*
They had a special <u>code of honor</u> **that was made for them.**

They had a special <u>code of honor</u> **which was made for them.**

places + *where, that,* or *which*
Hangzhou was a resort <u>town</u> **where people went for relaxation.**

Hangzhou was a resort <u>town</u> **that people went to for relaxation.**

Hangzhou was a resort <u>town</u> **which people went to for relaxation.**

time or period + *when* or *in which*
The Ming dynasty was a <u>time</u> **when people prospered.**

The 14th century was a <u>period</u> **in which Ife sculptors produced great art.**

Who, which, where or *when* are also used for nonrestrictive clauses. Nonrestrictive clauses do not define the noun. Instead, they add extra information about the noun that is not essential to the sentence.
Example: Ife sculptors made beautiful terra-cotta work, which is now in the British Museum. The Ming dynasty lasted until 1644, when the Qing dynasty began.

Combine these sentences into one complex sentence by using an adjective clause.

1. *Metropolis* is a 1919 German silent film.
   It showed a terrible vision of the future.

   "Metropolis" is a 1919 German silent film that showed a

   terrible vision of the future.

2. Metropolis, the city of the future, has an underground prison city.
   Workers live and work in the underground prison city.

3. The Masters of Metropolis rule the machines.
   The machines control the workers.

   _____

   _____

4. This was an age of cruelty.
   People were suffering in this age of cruelty.

   _____

   _____

5. The son of one of the Masters falls in love with a worker girl.
   The worker girl helps the workers to revolt against the Masters.

   _____

   _____

6. Fritz Lang was the great film director.
   Fritz Lang directed *Metropolis*.

   _____

   _____

2. Present Unreal Conditionals

One use of the **present unreal conditional** tense is to describe a situation that has never happened and can never happen. (See Unit 8, page 153 for the other use of this tense.)

if + simple past + conditional (*would* + base form)
If I **lived** in the future, I **would reside** on the planet Mars.

You can also use this conditional when the *if*-clause is not explicitly stated in a sentence, but is understood.

If I **lived** in the future, I **would be** able to see how the world resolves its problems. I **would see** the growth of new technology. I **would be** part of a new world.

Complete the paragraph by writing the correct form of the verb in parentheses. Use the present, simple past, or conditional.

The World I Want to Live In

For me, the future will be a difficult time if changes are not made today.

Some problems like poverty, violence, and pollution _____ *(be)* part of
1

our present world. But if I _____ *(be)* able to create a perfect world,
2

everyone _____ *(have)* a clean and safe place to live, and the planet
3

_____ *(not / suffer)* from contamination. If we _____ *(live)* in a
4   5

just and merciful world, people _____ *(want)* everyone to have the
6

necessities of life. In my perfect world, selfishness would be banished.

E. Preparing the Final Draft

*Reread your second draft and correct any errors you find. Put a check (✓) in each
space as you edit for these points. Then write your corrected final version.*

> ### CHECKLIST FOR EDITING THE SECOND DRAFT
> _____ **adjective clauses**
> _____ **present unreal conditionals**

Additional Writing Opportunities

Write about one of the following topics.

1. Did you enjoy studying history in school? Why or why not? Write about how history could be made more interesting for students. Be sure to support your opinion with explanations, examples, and/or personal stories.

2. Write about the history of your family in past generations. Describe how they lived and the society they were a part of. Explain what work they did and what aspirations they had. What would they think of your life today?

3. Read a science fiction book or a story about the future. Then write an essay explaining the author's vision of the future. What was the main idea? Did it include a warning about our society? Could this future society really happen? Why or why not? Include your opinion of the book in the conclusion of your essay.

   Some science fiction novels are:
   1984, by George Orwell
   Brave New World, by Aldous Huxley
   The Time Machine, by H.G.Wells
   The Handmaid's Tale, by Margaret Atwood
   The Martian Chronicles and *Fahrenheit 451*, both by Ray Bradbury

4. Write an essay in which you describe your perfect world. Explain why it is ideal using details about the environment, society, art, etc.

5 THE HAPPIEST SCHOOL IN THE WORLD

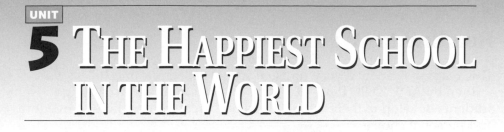

WRITING A CLASSIFICATION ESSAY

In this unit you will practice:
- classifying information
- writing a thesis statement for a classification essay
- giving examples in body paragraphs

Editing focus:
- parallel structure
- quantifiers: *one of* many

I Fluency Practice: A School Schedule

Imagine living in a perfect world where you can learn anything you want, for example, how to make films, write mystery novels, play drums, paint, dance, etc.

Fill in the school schedule below with the subjects you would like to study, regardless of their economic usefulness. When you have finished, share your schedule with a partner.

Time	Monday	Tuesday	Wednesday	Thursday	Friday

Reading for Writing

This reading is about a very unusual school called Summerhill. It was written by A. S. Neill (1883–1973), the school's founder. According to Neill, students develop to their full potential only in an atmosphere of freedom and personal choice.

SUMMERHILL: A RADICAL APPROACH TO CHILD REARING

by A. S. Neill

A.S. Neill hugging a student

This is a story of a modern school. Summerhill was founded in the year 1921. The school is in the village of Leiston in England, about 100 miles from
5 London. Some children come to Summerhill at five years old and others as late as fifteen. The children generally remain at the school until they are sixteen years old. They are housed by age
10 groups with a housemother for each group. The boys and girls live two, three, or four to a room. The pupils do not have room inspection and no one picks up after them. They are left free. No one tells
15 them what to wear: they put on any type of clothes they want to at any time.

What is Summerhill like? Well, for one thing, lessons are optional.[1] Children can go to them or stay away from them—for years if they want to. There *is* a timetable—but only for the teachers. No pupil is compelled[2]
20 to attend lessons. But if Jimmy comes to English on Monday and does not make an appearance again until Friday of the following week, the others quite rightly object that he is holding back the work, and they may throw him out for impeding[3] their progress. The children have classes usually according to their age, but sometimes according to their interests.
25 We have no new methods of teaching because we do not consider that teaching in itself matters very much. Whether a school has or doesn't have a special method for teaching long division is of no significance, because long division is of no importance except to those who want to learn it. And the child who wants to learn long division will learn it, no
30 matter how it is taught.

---

1. *optional:* by choice, voluntary
2. *compelled:* forced, obligated
3. *impeding:* blocking, obstructing

Obviously, a school that makes active children sit at desks studying mostly useless subjects is a bad school. It is a good school only for those uncreative citizens who want docile,[4] conformist children who will fit into a civilization whose standard of success is money. I had taught in ordinary
35 schools for years. I knew the other way well.

Children from other schools that come to Summerhill often say they will never attend any more lessons. They play and ride their bicycles and get in people's way, but they won't go to classes. This goes on for months. The recovery time is proportionate to the hatred their last school gave
40 them. Our record case was a girl who loafed[5] for three years. The average period of recovery from lesson aversion is three months. All the same, there is a lot of learning in Summerhill. Perhaps a group of our twelve-year-olds cannot compete with a class of equal age in handwriting or spelling or fractions. But in any competition requiring originality, our lot
45 would win.

A few years ago, someone at a General School Meeting (at which all school rules and punishments are voted on by the entire school, each pupil and each teacher having one vote) proposed that a certain student should be punished by being banned[6] from lessons for a week. The other
50 children protested on the grounds that the punishment was too severe.[7]

Summerhill is possibly the happiest school in the world. We have no truants[8] and seldom a case of homesickness. We very rarely have fights—quarrels, of course, but seldom have I seen a stand-up fight like the ones we used to have as boys. I seldom hear a child cry because
55 children when free have much less hate to express than children who are downtrodden.[9] Hate breeds hate, and love breeds love. Love means approving of children, and that is essential in any school. You can't be on the side of children if you punish them and yell at them. Summerhill is a school where the child knows he is approved of.
60 The function of the child is to live his own life, not the life that his parents think he should live, nor a life according to the educator who thinks he knows what is best. All this interference and guidance on the part of adults only produces a generation of robots.[10]

---

4. *docile:* manageable, obedient, submissive
5. *loaf:* to be lazy
6. *banned:* forbidden, excluded
7. *severe:* harsh, cruel, strict
8. *truants:* children who stay away from school without permission
9. *downtrodden:* oppressed, persecuted
10. *robots:* machines that perform the actions of a person

A. General Understanding

1. What Happens at Summerhill?

Read these situations and decide if they would occur at Summerhill. Write "Yes" or "No" and explain your answers in your notebook. Share them with a partner.

_____ 1. Students can wear whatever they like.

_____ 2. A girl breaks a window while playing ball and is yelled at and punished by a teacher.

_____ 3. Students choose what they want to learn.

_____ 4. A pupil goes to school only on Mondays.

_____ 5. Students are given low grades if their handwriting is not neat.

_____ 6. Each child must study a musical instrument because the school emphasizes the fine arts.

_____ 7. A servant comes to take a rich student home every afternoon in a Rolls Royce.

_____ 8. Teachers have a special hands-on method of teaching science.

2. The Main Idea and Your Response

Summarize A. S. Neill's main idea in your own words and write your opinion of Summerhill on the lines provided. Would you like to be a student there? Do you agree with the school's philosophy? All of it? Some of it? None of it? Read your opinion to a partner.

_____

_____

_____

_____

_____

_____

_____

_____

_____

_____

_____

B. Working with Language

1. Describing Summerhill and Ordinary Schools

Put these words from the reading on pages 78–79 under the category they describe: Summerhill or Ordinary Schools.

conformist	creative	docile	fights	free
loaf	obedient	playful	quarrel	robots

Ordinary Schools	Summerhill
conformist	

2. The Author's Purpose: Criticizing Ordinary Schools and Society

Most schools support the values of their surrounding society. In contrast, Summerhill challenges some of the values of modern society. What aspects of modern society does Summerhill challenge? Explain your answer with examples from the reading.

_____

_____

_____

_____

3. Finding Synonyms

For each bold word, underline the synonym (the word with a similar meaning.) Some of the bolded words may have more than one synonym. Compare your answers with a partner's.

1. **docile**   <u>obedient</u>   rebellious   <u>submissive</u>

2. **banned**   allowed   attacked   forbidden

3. **compelled**   coaxed   required   obligated

4. **impede**   restrict   hinder   block

5. **oppressed**   respected   depressed   downtrodden

6. **optional**   compulsory   free   by choice

7. **severe**   harsh   kind   desperate

4. The Principles of Summerhill

Complete this summary of some of the principles of Summerhill based on the writings of Erich Fromm, a noted psychologist. Use the bolded synonyms below and put verbs in the correct tense. Then, in your notebook, write a paragraph explaining which principles you agree or disagree with. Compare your answers with a partner's.

ban   compel   docile   impede   oppressed   optional   severe

1. The aim of education, like the aim of life, is for people to work joyfully and to find happiness, not to become _docile_ robots.
   _{obedient}

2. Education must be adapted to the psychological needs and abilities of the child. A child should not be _____ to change so that he or she fits the school; instead, the school should try to meet his or her needs.
   _{forced}

3. Rigidly imposed discipline and _____ punishment create fear; fear creates hostility in a child. This hostility may not be conscious, but it can deeply affect a child's future. Too much disciplining of children is harmful and obstructs their development.
   _{harsh}

4. Freedom doesn't mean you can do what you want. A teacher should not use force against a child; a child should not use force against a teacher. Violence is _____.
   _{not allowed}

5. Teachers should never lie to their students. Dishonesty _____ the educational process.
   _{interferes with}

6. The child should learn to face the world as an individual. He or she must not be _____.
   _{downtrodden}

III ◆ Prewriting Activities

A. The U.S. Educational System

Work in a small group. Look at this chart and answer the questions below about the U.S. educational system.

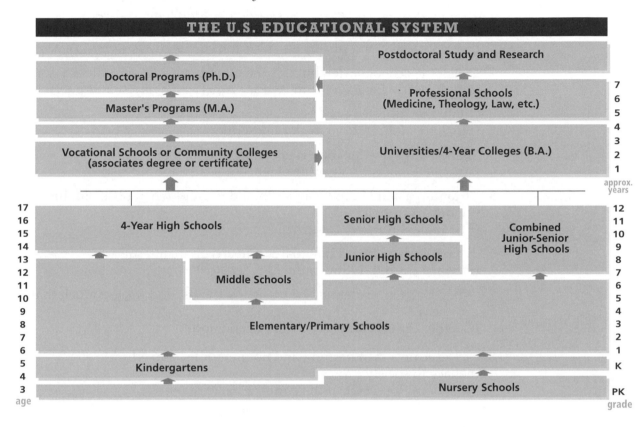

1. At what age do children usually begin elementary/primary school? middle school? a four-year high school?

2. How long does it take to get a diploma from a senior high school?

3. About how long does it take to get a bachelor's degree? a master's?

4. What higher degrees can one earn after a bachelor's degree?

B. Interpreting Quotes

Write a sentence in your notebook explaining the meaning of each quote. Compare your answers with a partner's.

1. "A student is not a vessel to be filled but a lamp to be lighted."
(Russian proverb)

   This statement means that students aren't mere objects to be filled with facts. The aim of education is to spark students' own creativity and ability to think for themselves.

2. "I pay the schoolmaster, but it is the other boys who educate my son."
(Ralph Waldo Emerson, 19th-century American essayist and poet)

3. "Only the educated are free."
(Epictetus, 1st-century Greek philosopher)

4. "Nine-tenths of education is encouragement."
(Anatole France, 19th-century French novelist and satirist)

5. "Train up a child in the way he should go, and when he is old, he will not depart from it."
(The Bible; Proverbs 22:6)

6. "Education is a better safeguard of liberty than an army."
(Edward Everett, 19th-century U.S. senator)

7. "They teach in academies far too many things, and far too much that is useless."
(Goethe, 18th-century German poet and author)

8. "To educate a man in mind and not in morals is to educate a menace to society."
(Theodore Roosevelt, 20th-century U.S. President)

C. Classification

Write the number of each quote from this page under the category it fits best: Freedom, The Meaning of Education, or Morality. Compare your answers with a partner's. Then discuss which quote you agree with most and why.

Freedom	The Meaning of Education	Morality
	1	

IV Structured Writing Focus

YOUR TASK

Write a five-paragraph classification essay about different types of teachers or students you have known.

ALTERNATIVE TASK: Write a five-paragraph classification essay about another group of people, such as family, friends, or coworkers. Divide them into categories and describe their similarities or differences.

A. Starting to Write

1. Before You Brainstorm

Read this classification essay and answer the questions on the next page.

Classifying Thinkers

We don't really know how to define intelligence. However, this does not discourage some people from categorizing others according to their intelligence or lack of it. In his essay, "Thinking as a Hobby," author William S. Golding[1] does exactly this. Golding divides people into three categories: grade-three thinkers, grade-two thinkers, and grade-one thinkers.

According to Golding, 90 percent of the population represents the largest category, called grade-three thinkers. These people are docile. They follow orders and obey other people's wishes. They never learn to think for themselves and cannot distinguish truth from lies. A dictator could take control of them and make them do whatever he wanted, as if they were sheep. The resulting mob would be brutal and ugly.

Grade-two thinkers, Golding's second category, are less likely to be influenced by a dictator. These grade-two thinkers, who make up 9 percent of the population, see corruption in the world. For example, grade-two thinkers may question the honesty of religious or political institutions. But while they find corruption in established institutions, they fail to find new ideals to believe in.

continued

---

1. William S. Golding (1911–1993) was the author of *Lord of the Flies,* a novel in which boys shipwrecked on an island fight a nightmarish war for power. Golding received the Nobel Prize in literature in 1983.

The remaining 1 percent of the population are what Golding calls grade-one thinkers. They not only see corruption, but they also know how to seek truth. Their lives are defined by wisdom, beauty, and knowledge. Such thinkers are creative and imaginative geniuses, like Mozart, Michelangelo, and Einstein, who opened new worlds in music, art, and science.

Michelangelo's *The Delphic Sibyl*

One wonders in which category Golding would place himself. Surely not among the "sheep"! Golding may prefer to believe that intelligence prevents people in the top tenth percentile of the population from following political dictators, but the number of doctors, teachers, lawyers, and writers in many countries who were willing supporters of Hitler, Stalin, and Mao shows that this belief is incorrect. In fact, sometimes the common sense and compassion of the ordinary man is all that stands between civilization and barbarism. As one of the so-called sheep, I say bah to Mr. Golding!

1. Circle the thesis statement. How does Golding classify people?

2. Underline the topic sentence of each body paragraph.

3. How does the author describe 90 percent of the population? the remaining 9 percent? the final 1 percent?

4. Underline the examples used in the third body paragraph to describe "grade-one thinkers."

5. What is the writer's opinion of Golding's essay? In which paragraph do you find this opinion?

6. What support (facts, examples) are used in the conclusion to argue the writer's point-of-view?

We **classify** information (we put similar objects or concepts into groups) using **a principle of classification** (the common similarity that the objects in the group share). Classification is necessary to understand all subjects, such as the arts, sciences, and business.

The topics below have been divided into several categories. Working with a partner, cross out the category that does not fit with the others. Decide what the categories have in common, and write that principle of classification.

1. Topic: **People**   monolingual, bilingual, ~~intelligent~~, multilingual

Principle of classification: <u>the number of languages a person speaks</u>

2. Topic: **Schools**   middle, private, elementary, secondary

Principle of classification: _____

3. Topic: **Teachers**   experienced, friendly, indifferent, hostile

Principle of classification: _____

4. Topic: **Subjects**   biology, physics, chemistry, history

Principle of classification: _____

5. Topic: **People**   athletes, artists, hard workers, scientists

Principle of classification: _____

2. Brainstorming

In your notebook, classify people from one of these groups. Consider these questions to help you classify.

Teachers
Have any teachers played an important role in your life? Did they have a positive or negative influence on you?

What were these teachers' attitudes toward their students?

Did the teachers make their material interesting?

Students

Do you remember the children or adolescents you went to school with?

Were there cliques of kids such as "popular" or "smart" kids? Where did you belong?

Was there a lot of teasing? bullying? rivalry among the groups?

FOR THE ALTERNATIVE TASK

Family

Can you group the people in your family according to their personalities? habits? How they react to family crises? How they get along?

Friends

Do you have different groups or categories of friends? friends to go out with? friends from work? from childhood? new friends? old friends?

Coworkers

What kinds of people do you know at work? Do you like them? admire them? fear them? How do they react to pressure or criticism from the boss?

3. The Introductory Paragraph

What is your topic? _____

What is your principle of classification? _____

4. The Body Paragraphs

Name your categories. Then, under each one, write descriptions of people belonging to that category. If you need more space, use your notebook. You do not need to write in complete sentences. Don't worry about grammar.

Category 1	Category 2	Category 3

5. The Conclusion

Write more notes in your notebook, answering these questions.

1. What is your opinion of the people in the different categories? Do you prefer one group to others? If so, why?

2. Is the information in your essay important for readers to know? Why?

B. Preparing the First Draft

1. Writing a Thesis Statement for a Classification Essay

A thesis statement for a classification essay can be written in two ways:

By giving the number of categories.
Golding divides **people into three categories:** grade-three thinkers, grade-two thinkers, and grade-one thinkers.

By giving the principle of classification.
Golding divides people **according to their intellectual ability:** grade-three thinkers, grade-two thinkers, and grade-one thinkers.

Write a thesis statement, describing the three categories for each of these topics. Use the classification expressions below. Write your sentences in your notebook and compare them with a partner's.

1. Topic: **Teachers**   friendly, unfriendly, indifferent

   There are three kinds of teachers: friendly teachers, unfriendly teachers, and indifferent teachers.

2. Topic: **Friends**   childhood friends, friends from school, friends from work

3. Topic: **Family**   my family in New York, my family in Miami, my family in Cuba

EXPRESSIONS USED FOR CLASSIFICATION

Teachers can be	**categorized**	in three ways/groups
	classified	in three ways/groups
	grouped	in three ways
	VERBS	

There are three different	**categories**	of teachers
	classes	
	kinds	
	types	
	groups	
	NOUNS	

2. Topic Sentences

Your classification essay should have a topic sentence for each body paragraph. The topic sentence announces the category that the body paragraph describes.

The first category consists of	inspired teachers who make their subject come alive.
The next group includes	average teachers who communicate information, but don't inspire their students.
The last category is made up of	unsatisfactory teachers who don't help their students learn.

3. Body Paragraphs: Giving Examples

Remember to give examples in the body paragraphs to make your classification convincing and interesting to others. Use classification expressions such as the ones bolded in the following paragraphs.

Read each paragraph. After reading each one, write the details you remember about it in your notebook without looking at the paragraph. Write in your own words. When you are done, compare your notes with the paragraph.

Body Paragraph 1

The first category of teachers I have had are inspired teachers who make their subject come alive. Mrs. Nash, who taught me to love playing the piano, **is an example.** She was never too busy to listen. Once I told her that I liked popular music better than the classical pieces she always had me practice. From then on, at the end of the lesson, she always included one popular song that I could play for my friends. She also complimented me whenever I had worked hard on a piece. She helped me develop as a musician and showed me the joy of playing a musical instrument.

Body Paragraph 2

I have had many **average teachers,** who communicate information but don't inspire their students. Mr. Wilson **is one example of this category.** He did his duty as a teacher, but never did more than what was necessary. He gave us a good textbook and clear lessons, but he rarely tried to make his material exciting. I was very jealous of students in the other history class who were doing a computer re-enactment of a Civil War battle. With Mr. Wilson, we only memorized dates and places. He taught us well enough to pass our exams, but he never inspired us.

Body Paragraph 3

   Mrs. Rinehart **is typical of those unsatisfactory teachers** who don't help their students learn. She gave the same lectures year after year and never noticed that the students were sleeping. Perhaps she knew and didn't care. Her exams sometimes included questions that were not in the textbook or had not been discussed in class. When we complained, she would say, "Oh? Well, you should know it anyway." She was indifferent to us and to the material. She didn't care if we learned anything at all.

4. Conclusion

In most essays, the writer's idea or opinion appears in the thesis statement in the introduction. However, in a classification essay, the thesis statement mentions only the categories that the writer will discuss. The writer's opinion appears in the conclusion.

5. Organizing Your Essay

Study this block diagram of a five-paragraph essay to plan a first draft of your essay. In your notebook, draw your own diagram and write your notes in each of its sections.

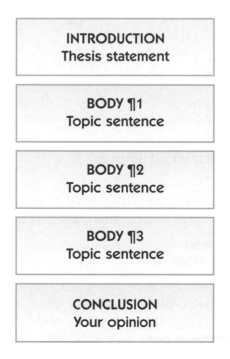

*Write a **first draft** of your essay. Remember to write in complete sentences and try to use some of the vocabulary and structures that you have practiced in this unit.*

C. Revising the First Draft

When you have finished writing your first draft, read it to a partner.

CHECKLIST FOR REVISING THE FIRST DRAFT

When you listen to your partner's essay and when you consider your own, keep these questions in mind:

1. Is the topic divided into three clear, separate categories?

2. Is the thesis statement clear?

3. Does each body paragraph discuss a different category and start with a topic sentence?

4. Are there enough examples to make the essay interesting? convincing? Are classification expressions used?

5. Does the conclusion give the writer's opinion?

After discussing your essay with a partner, you may want to reorganize your categories or add examples.

*Now write a **second draft** that includes all additions and changes.*

D. Editing the Second Draft

After you have written a second draft, proofread your work for any errors and correct them. These guidelines and exercises should help.

1. Parallel Structure

Parallel structure means that all words, phrases, or sentences joined by *and, or, but,* or a comma must be equal grammatical units.

Incorrect (Not Parallel)	**Correct (Parallel)**
Teachers can be classified into three categories: **those who make class interesting, useful lessons, and those who bore their students.**	Teachers can be classified into three categories: **those who make class interesting, those who teach useful lessons, and those who bore their students.**
(CLAUSE, ADJECTIVE + NOUN, CLAUSE)	(CLAUSE, CLAUSE, CLAUSE)

Incorrect (Not Parallel)	Correct (Parallel)
Patience and **dedicated** are two qualities of good teachers. (NOUN, ADJECTIVE)	**Patience** and **dedication** are two qualities of good teachers. (NOUN, NOUN)
Good students study **regularly** and **efficient.** (ADVERB, ADJECTIVE)	Good students study **regularly** and **efficiently.** (ADVERB, ADVERB)
A student's dream is **to learn** and **growing.** (INFINITIVE, GERUND)	A student's dream is **to learn** and **to grow.** (INFINITIVE, INFINITIVE)

Complete the following sentences with parallel structures. Use your imagination. Then share your answers with a partner.

1. The students in my history class fall into three groups: those who study a lot, _____, and those who do not study at all.

2. Our teacher sometimes starts to lose his patience and begins _____ when dealing with the students who do no studying at all.

3. Some students don't really want to go to school. Their goal is to go home and _____.

4. As a result, our teacher becomes uncomfortable and _____ when he has to deal with them.

5. He wants to ignore them and _____ that they are not there.

6. Teachers would like to have students who respond eagerly and _____ to everything they say, but they also have to teach students who do not.

Read this summary of an essay by Ada Louise Huxtable.[1] If the words in bold are parallel with the other words in the sentences, put a check (✓) above them. If they are not, cross them out and rewrite them using parallel structures. There are five more mistakes. Compare your answers with a partner's.

A Critique of Clutter

Architecture critic Ada Louise Huxtable writes in an essay called "Modern-Life Battle: Conquering Clutter" that there are three types of people in this world: those who clutter[2] compulsively, those who **clutter** intentionally, ~~with intention~~, and those who throw things away irrationally. The first category consists of people who clutter compulsively. They are passionate and **enthusiastically** collectors who have to buy everything they see. After a while, they cannot distinguish between valuable objects and **objects that are worthless**. The members of the second group, those who clutter intentionally, are quite different. These people collect with the eyes of decorators and **art**. Their clutter reflects their aesthetic **ideals** and their financial investments. The last category is made up of those people who throw things away irrationally. They are against buying and **collect** things. Huxtable says they live in "sleek and shining rooms, with every perfect thing in its perfect place." In her opinion, the members of this category are ignoring their needs and **forget** their identities. One thing is certain: No matter which group you belong to, the most important thing you need to know is who you are. If you know this much, you will not let your possessions possess you!

---

1. Ada Louise Huxtable (1921–present) is an American architectural critic who wrote for *The New York Times* from 1963 to 1982. Huxtable received a Pulitzer Prize for her distinguished criticism in 1970.
2. *clutter:* to crowd a room with objects in disorder

2. Quantifiers: *One of* Many

The pronoun *one* is a **singular** subject. *One of* always means one of a group. *One of* is usually followed by a **plural** noun and a **singular** verb.

Incorrect
One of the teachers <u>are</u> friendly.

One of my friends <u>study</u> art.

Correct
One of the teachers <u>is</u> friendly.

One of my friends <u>studies</u> art.

Do not leave off the plural ending of a plural group:

Incorrect
One of the <u>child</u> is painting.

Stanford is **one of** the best <u>university</u> in the United States.

Correct
One of the <u>children</u> is painting.

Stanford is **one of** the best <u>universities</u> in the United States.

Read these paragraphs. If the words and phrases in bold are correct, put a check (✓) above them. If they are incorrect, cross them out and rewrite them. There are four more mistakes. Compare your answers with a partner's.

I have fond memories of ~~one of my high school math teacher.~~ *one of my high school math teachers.* Her name was Rosemary O'Toole, and she made me aware of my potential to be a good math student. I was intimidated by the other math students at first, but because of my teacher's encouragement, I received **one of the highest grade** in the class at the end of the year. In fact, **one of the math awards were** given to me at the end of the year for my grades. Without her kind attention, I would never have achieved such grades or understood the mysteries of calculus.

There is no doubt in my mind that **one of a good teacher's abilities are** the ability to motivate his or her students. It is not **one of the skills** that teachers learn in teacher training courses. However, one thing is certain: students learn faster and better when their teachers have time to treat them as individuals and not as **one of many person** in the class.

E. Preparing the Final Draft

Reread your second draft and correct any errors you find. Put a check (✓) in each space as you edit for these points. Then write your corrected final version.

CHECKLIST FOR EDITING THE SECOND DRAFT

_____ **parallel structures**

_____ **quantifiers:** *one of* many

V ▸ Additional Writing Opportunities

Write about one of the following topics.

1. Explain the organization of the U.S. educational system to students from another country. You can refer to the chart on page 83 for your information. If you wish, include additional information that you want them to know.

2. Have you ever been to school in a country other than the United States, or do you know about the school system of another country? Compare the educational system in the United States with that of another country. Remember to discuss similarities as well as differences.

3. Write a five-paragraph classification essay about a subject you have studied in school. Some subjects you could write about that use classification systems are zoology (the study of animals), political science (the study of world governments), or film studies (the study of different types of films).

4. A good college should allow students to develop in many ways: academically, socially, culturally. Do you agree or disagree? To what extent does your college provide these opportunities? Write a five-paragraph essay expressing your opinion.

5. Write an essay explaining the meaning of the quote below. Do you agree or disagree with the quote? Discuss your opinion of it.

   "Without education, you're not going anywhere in this world."
   (Malcolm X, 20th-century American Civil Rights leader)

6 ARE YOU GETTING ENOUGH SLEEP?

WRITING A CAUSE-AND-EFFECT ESSAY

In this unit you will practice:

- categorizing research notes
- creating body paragraphs from research notes
- writing transitional sentences

Editing focus:

- subordinate clauses
- *because / because of*
- logical connectors
- fragments
- run-on sentences and comma splices

 ## Fluency Practice: Freewriting

How much sleep do you get at night? Do you get enough sleep? Why or why not? What happens to you when you don't sleep enough? Do you ever fall asleep during the day? When and where?

Write for ten minutes in answer to these questions. Try to express yourself as well as you can. Don't worry about mistakes. Share your writing with a partner.

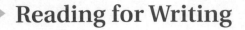

Reading for Writing

This essay discusses why people today don't get enough sleep.

THE CAUSES OF SLEEP DEPRIVATION IN AMERICA: A NATION OF WALKING ZOMBIES

When we operate a machine, we need to make sure that all of its parts are in good working order so that it will function efficiently. If we are careless, the machine will break down when we least expect it. The same can be said about the most complex of machines, the human body. When
5 the body is sleep-deprived,[1] it is like a car running on a half-empty gas tank. People usually don't know when their bodies will run out of fuel—and the results can be disastrous. In fact, sleep deprivation has caused tragedy: It is the second leading cause of all car accidents in the United States. At least one-third of Americans, about 85 million people, sleep
10 only six of the eight or nine hours that sleep specialists say is needed each night. According to James Maas, a sleep specialist, this situation has created "a nation of walking zombies."[2] If people slept eight hours, they would be less drowsy,[3] they would be more alert and productive at work, and they would have more creative and joyful lives. In addition, they
15 would have fewer accidents, making the world a safer place for us all. We clearly need to sleep more and educate people about the three major causes of sleep deprivation: modern technology, insomnia, and sleep apnea.

In our society, sleep
20 deprivation has developed along with advances in technology and our longer schedules. Before the invention of the light bulb,
25 people woke when the sun rose and went to sleep when the sun set. Today the division between daytime and nighttime is less clear. Because people
30 can work at night with the aid of artificial light, daytime is

---

1. *to be sleep-deprived:* to not get enough sleep
2. *zombies:* the walking dead in myth; people who behave like robots
3. *drowsy:* sleepy

no longer the only time when people can be awake and productive. Many people lead sleepy lives because they work night shifts at places such as hospitals and factories. In the past two decades, the computer, the fax
35 machine, and the cell phone have extended our schedules around the clock. In addition, our lives are filled with complex obligations both on the job and in the family, and sleep seems to be the first thing we sacrifice when we have too much to do. Although millions of years of biological evolution indicate that nighttime is a time for rest, many of us simply
40 ignore the rules of the natural sleep cycle.

In addition to technology, insomnia causes sleep deprivation. Insomnia is the psychological inability to fall or stay asleep. Insomnia can be divided into two categories: short-term insomnia, which is temporary, and long-term insomnia, which is a chronic condition. People who suffer from
45 stress due to a problem at home or pressure at work often develop short-term insomnia. People can also have short-term insomnia as a result of temporary environmental factors, such as living in a noisy environment, or from habits like drinking too much coffee and taking stimulants.[4] On the other hand, some people develop long-term insomnia from a chronic
50 condition, such as clinical depression.[5]

The third major cause of sleep deprivation is a physical problem rather than a psychological one. Approximately 20 million Americans suffer from sleep apnea, which is the most common physical disorder that prevents people from getting a good night's rest. Sleep apnea creates an
55 obstruction in the nose or throat that stops the sleeper from breathing for several seconds. The sleeper gasps for air to keep from choking and, therefore, rarely enjoys a deep sleep. Sleep apnea results in snoring—the most familiar symptom of this disorder. Only recently have scientists realized that snoring is not merely an individual's annoying sleep behavior,
60 but a sign of his or her difficulty in breathing and an indication that medical attention is needed.

Most Americans regard sleeping as a waste of time. This is the attitude that sleep specialists are trying to change. Many people are still unaware of the restorative[6] power of sleep. Although not everything is known about
65 sleep, doctors believe that it is essential for our physical and mental well-being. We need to reduce sleep deprivation, which is caused by 24-hour schedules, insomnia, and sleep apnea, because one person's sleepiness can result in the next person's tragedy.

---

4. *stimulants:* drugs that keep people awake
5. *clinical depression:* a medical condition of persistent, unrelieved sadness
6. *restorative:* healing

A. General Understanding

1. Understanding the Main Idea

Answer these questions and compare your answers with a partner's.

1. What is the main idea of the essay? Underline the thesis statement.

2. Underline one effect or result of sleep deprivation that is mentioned in the essay.

3. What recommendation for the future does the writer give in the conclusion? Underline the sentence that gives this advice.

2. Identifying Causes

Write on the lines below the three main causes (Social, Psychological, and Physical) of sleep deprivation discussed in the reading on pages 98–99. Match the topics on the left with the cause they are associated with. Put a check (✓) in the appropriate column.

	Cause 1: Social _____	Cause 2: Psychological _____	Cause 3: Physical _____
1. Snoring			
2. Stress at work			
3. Family arguments			
4. Artificial light			
5. Depression			
6. Shift work			
7. Gasping for air			

B. Working with Language

1. Crossword Puzzle

Working with a partner, complete this crossword puzzle. Use the clues in the Across and Down columns, and choose your answers from these bolded words.

alert	**deep**	**ignore**
awareness	**deprive**	**restorative**
categories	**environment**	**risk**
complex	**essential**	**symptom**
cycle	**function**	**well-being**

ACROSS
1. danger
5. sign or indication of a medical condition
6. wide awake
7. repeated sequence of events
9. surroundings
11. necessary
12. to not pay enough attention to
13. state of health and happiness

DOWN
1. refreshing, healing
2. to operate
3. divisions, classifications
4. consciousness
7. not simple
8. to prevent, deny
10. profound, intense

2. The Two Stages of Sleep

Using some of the words from the crossword puzzle, complete these paragraphs. The first letter of the correct word is given. When you have finished, compare your answers with a partner's.

People who **d**_____ themselves of a few hours of sleep every
1

night **i**_____ the importance of sleep. Their general **w**_____
2   3

is dangerously at **r**_____; they might miss out on both of the
4

necessary stages of sleep. Throughout the sleep **c**_____, sleepers
5

experience two stages of sleep: the first is the non-REM stage, in which

sleepers' slow rolling eye movements reflect a quiet, restful sleep; the

second is the REM stage, in which sleepers' rapid eye movements indicate

that they are dreaming and experiencing intense brain activity. During both

stages, people are not **a**_____; they are in a **d**_____ sleep.
6   7

The non-REM stage and the REM stage are both **e**_____ for
8

people's health. Both types of sleep are **r**_____ because each stage
9

helps people adjust to their **e**_____. Without having both kinds of
10

sleep, people do not **f**_____ well in the world.
11

3. Open for Discussion

Discuss these questions in a small group.

1. Are you tired often? What are the causes of your tiredness?

2. Have you ever felt like you were going to doze off when driving a car? What happened?

3. Did you ever not get enough sleep and, as a result, you didn't work as hard at school or on the job? Were you less motivated to work because you were tired?

4. What, if anything, can you change in your life to be less tired during the day?

III

Prewriting Activities

A. The Epworth Sleepiness Scale

Working in a small group, complete this poll created by the sleep expert Dr. Murray W. Johns. Then compare your answers with another group's.

The
Epworth
Sleepiness
Scale

Name: _____ Today's date: _____

Your age (yrs.): _____ Your sex (Male = M, Female = F): _____

How likely are you to doze off or fall asleep in the following situations, in contrast to feeling just tired?

This refers to your usual way of life in recent times.

Even if you haven't done some of these things recently, try to work out how they would have affected you.

Use the following scale to choose the most appropriate number for each situation:

0 = would never doze	**2** = moderate chance of dozing
1 = slight chance of dozing	**3** = high chance of dozing

It is important that you answer each question as best you can.

Situation	Chance of Dozing (0–3)
Sitting and reading	_____
Watching TV	_____
Sitting, inactive in a public place (e.g., a theater or meeting)	_____
As a passenger in a car for an hour without a break	_____
Lying down to rest in the afternoon when circumstances permit	_____
Sitting and talking to someone	_____
Sitting quietly after lunch without alcohol	_____
In a car, while stopped for a few minutes in traffic	_____

B. Dream Theories

Dreaming is an essential part of sleep. Read about what the following people and texts say about dreams. Then write which theories you agree or disagree with in your notebook. Read your response to a partner and then discuss each other's opinions.

1. **Aristotle** (384–322 B.C.): a Greek philosopher who suggested that dreams are the result of physical disturbances, such as an upset stomach. He also believed that dreams contain memories of events that happened during the day.

2. **Religious writings,** such as the Bible and the Koran, sometimes describe dreams as symbols or visions of the future.

3. **Sigmund Freud**[1] (1856–1939): an Austrian psychoanalyst,[2] who thought dreams contain unconscious thoughts[3] and desires that are socially unacceptable. Freud believed that people need a psychoanalyst to help them understand their dreams.

Freud, bottom left and Jung, bottom right, with other psychologists

4. **Carl Jung**[4] (1875–1961): a Swiss psychologist who was one of Freud's students. Jung disagreed somewhat with Freud on the meaning of dreams. He did not believe that all dreams reflect unconscious desires. Jung also felt that people could learn to interpret their own dreams.

---

1. *Freud* is pronounced "Froyd"
2. *psychoanalyst:* a doctor who treats emotional disorders by having patients talk about their personal experiences, especially their early childhood and dreams
3. *unconscious thoughts:* thoughts that a person has but is unaware of, which are caused by fears and memories
4. *Jung* is pronounced "Yoong"

IV Structured Writing Focus

Write a five-paragraph cause-and-effect essay that describes what happens at work, at school, and on the road, when people don't get enough sleep. What are the consequences of sleep deprivation to society?

ALTERNATIVE TASK: Write a five-paragraph essay on your dreams: What kinds of dreams you have, what you think they symbolize, and what you think causes them.

A. Starting to Write

1. Brainstorming

Write notes for your essay in your notebook on these questions.

FOR THE MAIN TASK

What problems can people have when they don't get enough sleep? problems with concentration? memory? mood? motivation? health? difficulties at work? at school? on the road? What kinds of accidents could occur?

How can sleep deprivation harm society? public safety and health? job/school performance?

FOR THE ALTERNATIVE TASK

What types of dreams do you have most often? Which are the most vivid? Ones about falling? flying? being chased? traveling? dreams about water? storms? people from your present or past? people who are no longer alive?

What do you think your dreams represent? thoughts or desires? fear? avoiding a problem? ambition? loss of self-control? different parts of your personality? predictions about the future?

What do you think causes your dreams? psychological states? memories from the past? events that happened that day? physical problems (such as eating too much before you go to sleep)?

2. Categorizing Research Notes

Many essays are enhanced by research facts that appear in the body paragraphs to support the main idea. Take notes when you research from a text. Do not copy the exact words of the text unless you plan to quote it. Then categorize your research notes by topic to organize the information into paragraphs.

Put these student notes into three categories for three different body paragraphs.

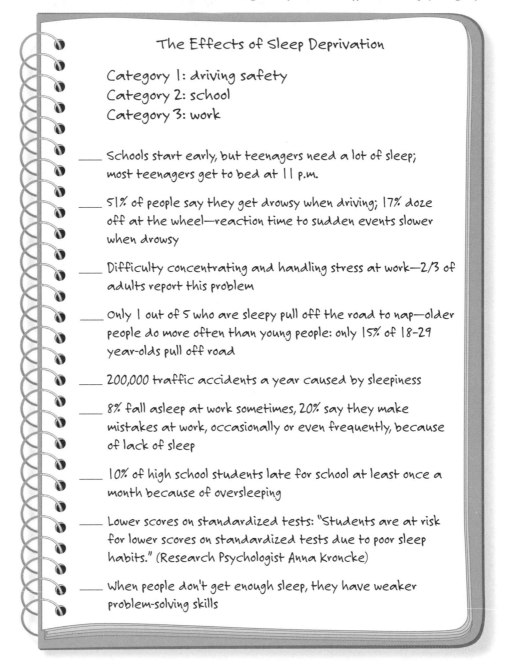

The Effects of Sleep Deprivation

Category 1: driving safety
Category 2: school
Category 3: work

____ Schools start early, but teenagers need a lot of sleep; most teenagers get to bed at 11 p.m.

____ 51% of people say they get drowsy when driving; 17% doze off at the wheel—reaction time to sudden events slower when drowsy

____ Difficulty concentrating and handling stress at work—2/3 of adults report this problem

____ Only 1 out of 5 who are sleepy pull off the road to nap—older people do more often than young people: only 15% of 18–29 year-olds pull off road

____ 200,000 traffic accidents a year caused by sleepiness

____ 8% fall asleep at work sometimes, 20% say they make mistakes at work, occasionally or even frequently, because of lack of sleep

____ 10% of high school students late for school at least once a month because of oversleeping

____ Lower scores on standardized tests: "Students are at risk for lower scores on standardized tests due to poor sleep habits." (Research Psychologist Anna Kroncke)

____ When people don't get enough sleep, they have weaker problem-solving skills

Source: (Except as indicated) National Sleep Foundation (NSF) 2000 Omnibus Sleep Poll

B. Preparing the First Draft

1. Creating Body Paragraphs from Research Notes

Read these notes that the student writer organized under category two, School. Then read the paragraph that the student created from the notes and answer the questions that follow.

Notes for Category Two: School

- Lower scores on standardized tests: "Students are at risk for lower scores on standardized tests due to poor sleep habits." (Research Psychologist Anna Kroncke)
- problem-solving skills weakened when people don't sleep enough
- Schools start early, teens need a lot of sleep; go to bed at 11 P.M.
- 10% of high school students late once a month—oversleeping

Paragraph

Not getting enough sleep can have a negative effect* on how well students do in school. According to a National Sleep Foundation Poll, 10 percent of high school students are late at least one day each month because they oversleep. They miss schoolwork and have difficulty catching up. I know this from personal experience. When I was in high school, I was always tired because I stayed up late talking to my friends. I really needed more time to sleep every morning, but school started early. So did the standardized tests! "Students are at risk for lower scores on standardized tests due to poor sleep habits," writes Research Psychologist Anna Kroncke. Students can't think as fast or solve problems as well if they don't get enough sleep the night before. Their whole school future could suffer because of a lack of sleep.

---

*The expression *to have a positive / negative effect on* (someone or something) can be used in a cause-and-effect essay to show good or bad results.

1. Underline the topic sentence in the paragraph.

2. Which sentence includes a quote? Why is a quote effective?

3. Which sentence includes statistics? Do the statistics support the idea in the topic sentence?

4. Which sentences describe a personal experience? Why do you think the writer added a personal experience?

5. Underline the concluding sentence. How does it reinforce the topic sentence?

2. Transitional Sentences

We use **transitional sentences** to connect the ideas from one paragraph to the next, to add ideas, or to show a change of topic. A transitional sentence often comes before the topic sentence. Sometimes the transitional sentence is the topic sentence of the paragraph.

Look back at the essay "The Causes of Sleep Deprivation in America" on pages 98–99. Underline the transitional sentences in the second and third body paragraphs. Are they the topic sentences of these paragraphs or not? Compare your answers with a partner's.

PRACTICE WITH TRANSITIONAL SENTENCES

Read these two paragraphs. On the lines provided write the sentence from the shaded box that would make a good transition to connect the paragraphs.

Modern technology has a negative effect on the environment. For example, because of modern technology, industrial pollution contaminates rivers and destroys forests and wildlife.

_____

_____

Modern technology has made it possible to genetically change food so that we can produce more of it. But genetically modified foods may be dangerous. Some people say these foods threaten the environment and destroy some birds and insects, including the Monarch butterfly.

TRANSITIONAL SENTENCES

a. In addition to industrial pollution, food modification endangers our environment.

b. It is short-sighted to worry about industrial pollution without considering the destruction of the Monarch butterfly.

c. Food has become very unnatural.

Working with a partner, read the two paragraphs below and connect them by writing your own transitional sentence for the beginning of the second paragraph.

Modern technology has surely simplified our lives. Today many modern appliances do in seconds what it used to take people hours to do. For instance, instead of working with pen and paper, we can now use a calculator to do our accounting. The computer has also transformed our lives by making information available to us in an instant.

_____

_____

Modern technology has led to sleep deprivation because it allows people to work more. It is not uncommon for people to work at home or late into the night. They sometimes even work while commuting. Because of this, many say that today's technology has added stress to their lives.

3. Organizing Your Essay

Study this block diagram of a five-paragraph essay to plan a first draft of your essay. In your notebook, draw your own diagram and write your ideas in each of its sections.

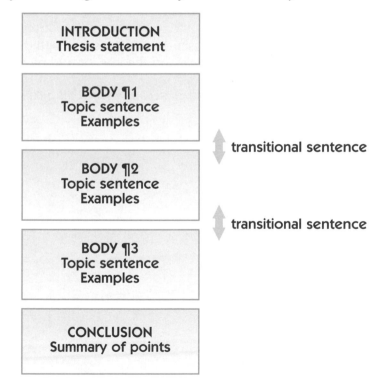

Review your notes and consider doing additional research, if needed. Then write a **first draft** *of your essay. Remember to write in complete sentences, and try to use some of the vocabulary and structures that you have practiced in this unit.*

C. Revising the First Draft

When you have finished writing your first draft, read it to a partner.

CHECKLIST FOR REVISING THE FIRST DRAFT

When you listen to your partner's essay and when you discuss your own, keep these questions in mind:

1. Does the introduction provide enough background information?

2. Is the thesis statement clear? For the main task, does it mention three effects that are supported by the body paragraphs?

3. For the alternative task, do the body paragraphs describe your dreams, what they symbolize, and what causes them?

4. Are there appropriate examples in each body paragraph? Are the transitions between body paragraphs logical?

5. Does the conclusion refer to the idea in the thesis statement? For the alternative task, does it suggest the writer's opinion about the meaning or importance of dreams?

After discussing your essay with a partner, you may want to reorganize your ideas, omit some, or add new ones.

*Now write a **second draft** that includes all of your additions and changes.*

D. Editing the Second Draft

After you have written a second draft, proofread your work for any errors and correct them. These guidelines and exercises should help.

1. Subordinate Clauses

We often use **subordinate clauses** to show cause and effect. A subordinate clause is always attached to a main clause and contains a subject and a verb. It starts with a **subordinator**, such as *because* or *since*. When a subordinate clause starts a sentence, a comma is necessary.

Cause	Effect
because + subject + verb	
Because he was deprived of sleep,	his test scores suffered.
Since he was deprived of sleep,	his test scores suffered.
SUBORDINATE CLAUSE	MAIN CLAUSE

When the main clause starts the sentence, no comma is needed.

His test scores suffered **because** he was deprived of sleep.
MAIN CLAUSE   SUBORDINATE CLAUSE

Using these cues, write two sentences with subordinate clauses that contain because *and* since.

1. workers are tired / could easily make mistakes

   Since workers are tired, they could easily make mistakes.

   Workers could easily make mistakes because they are tired.

2. the jet plane takes us great distances in a short time / we can sometimes see the sun rise more than once in a day

   _____

   _____

3. people are stressed / they have trouble relaxing

   _____

   _____

2. *Because / Because of*

Because and *because of* both show cause and effect but use different sentence structures.

because + subject + verb
Because we lack sleep, we are often impatient and irritable.

because of + noun
Because of a lack of sleep, we are often impatient and irritable.

Because of can also come after the main clause, but no comma is needed.

We are often impatient and irritable **because of** a lack of sleep.

Use these cues to create sentences with because *or* because of. *After you have finished, compare your answers with a partner's.*

1. have too many things to do / they sleep less

   Because people have too many things to do, they sleep less.

2. sleep deprivation / many students are late to school

   Many students are late to school because of sleep deprivation.

3. lack sleep / people are more likely to catch colds

   _____

4. have difficulty sleeping / some people become depressed

   _____

5. are drowsy / people may have more accidents at work

   _____

6. artificial light / people sometimes work at night instead of sleeping

   _____

7. stress and environmental factors / some people develop short-term insomnia.

   _____

3. Logical Connectors

Logical connectors are adverbs or conjunctions that link sentences. Some logical connectors also express cause and effect. Except for *so*, which follows a comma, these logical connectors follow a semi-colon or start a sentence.

Cause	Effect

He was deprived of sleep**; consequently,** his test scores suffered.

He was deprived of sleep**; as a result,** his test scores suffered.

He was deprived of sleep**; therefore,** his test scores suffered.

He was deprived of sleep**. Thus,** his test scores suffered.

He was deprived of sleep**, so** his test scores suffered.

LOGICAL CONNECTORS

Use the cues to write two sentences. For each sentence use one of the logical connectors in parentheses.

1. lack of sleep weakens people's bodies / they are more likely to get sick *(as a result / therefore)*

   Lack of sleep weakens people's bodies; therefore, they are more likely to get sick.

   Lack of sleep weakens people's bodies; as a result, they are more likely to get sick.

2. modern technology allows us to work 24 hours a day / we work more and have less time for sleep *(as a result / consequently)*

3. modern technology has given us more options in our lives / it is more difficult to make decisions *(thus / therefore)*

4. Fragments

A **sentence** has one or more subjects, a complete verb, and a complete idea.

A **fragment** is *not* a complete sentence. It may contain a subject and a verb, but it does not have a complete idea. Fragments are not acceptable in formal writing.

Fragments (Incorrect)	Sentences (Correct)
Despite Bruno's intelligence.	Despite Bruno's intelligence, he didn't do well at school.
Because Bruno was always tired.	Because Bruno was always tired, he fell asleep in class and didn't learn the material.
Although Bruno tried hard.	Although Bruno tried hard, he couldn't stay awake for our test.
After the test was over and we went to the party.	After the test was over and we went to the party, he was still as sleepy as ever.

Correct this story by crossing out the fragments that you find and then connecting them to the sentences to which they belong. There are six more error. When you have finished, compare your answers with a partner's.

Thanks to the Advice of a Friend

Because of his snoring, Roger Smith recently faced the possibility of living a very lonely life. ~~Although he had been an active Boy Scout leader for years. His snoring made him stop doing this important volunteer work for the community a year ago.~~ Although he had been an active Boy Scout leader for years, his snoring made him stop doing this important volunteer work for the community a year ago.

After an overnight stay with the Scouts and their fathers in a big canvas tent. Everyone laughed at him at breakfast the next morning. Although they all had great respect for him. His snoring had made him an object of ridicule. Because he couldn't bear the thought of ever being laughed at again. He resigned from his position two weeks later. Despite his ability to help others. Roger had no way of helping himself. Because of this incident. Roger started to lose confidence in himself and turned his back on scouting.

After he explained his problem to a friend. Roger was able to turn his life around. His friend sent him to a doctor that specialized in sleep disorders. By means of a mechanical device, which the doctor prescribed, Roger now has "continuous positive airway pressure" when he sleeps. As a result, he no longer snores.

5. Run-on Sentences and Comma Splices

A **run-on sentence** is two distinct sentences incorrectly run together as one. A **comma splice** is two distinct sentences incorrectly connected with a comma. Run-on sentences and comma splices are not acceptable in formal writing.

Run-on sentence
My father was very practical he didn't take my dreams too seriously.

Comma splice
My father was very practical, he didn't take my dreams too seriously.

Run-on sentences and comma splices can be corrected in several ways:

1. By separating the sentences with a semi-colon.

   My father was very practical; he didn't take my dreams too seriously.

2. By separating the sentences with a semi-colon and a logical connector.

   My father was very practical; **therefore,** he didn't take my dreams too seriously.

3. By separating the sentences with a comma and a conjunction.

   My father was very practical, **and** he didn't take my dreams too seriously.

4. By separating the sentences with a period.

   My father was very practical. He didn't take my dreams too seriously.

5. By making one of the sentences a subordinate clause.

   Because my father was very practical, he didn't take my dreams too seriously.

   My father didn't take my dreams too seriously **because he was very practical.**

Read these sentences and put a check (✓) next to those that are correct.
Put an X next to those that are run-on sentences or comma splices and correct
them. After you have finished, compare your answers with a partner's.

___X___ 1. I remember my dreams I always write them down.

I remember my dreams because I always write them down.

_____ 2. Although Freud and Jung disagreed about why people dream,
they agreed that dreams are a very important part of people's lives.

_____

_____

_____ 3. Freud insisted that dreams should be interpreted as unfulfilled
and forbidden desires, this theory was not acceptable to Jung.

_____

_____

_____ 4. Jung believed that people could interpret their dreams if they
followed his strategies.

_____

_____

_____ 5. Freud believed that we dream in order to defend ourselves from
the stress of daily life, he thought if we did not dream, everyday
life would be intolerable.

_____

_____

_____ 6. Freud thought that dreams are not random events; they all have
causes.

_____

_____

E. Preparing the Final Draft

Reread your second draft and correct any errors you find. Put a check (✓) in each space as you edit for these points. Then write your corrected final version.

CHECKLIST FOR EDITING THE SECOND DRAFT

_____ **subordinate clauses**

_____ *because / because of*

_____ **logical connectors**

_____ **fragments**

_____ **run-on sentences and comma splices**

 # Additional Writing Opportunities

Write about one of the following topics.

1. Have you ever been tired at a certain time in your life? Write an essay about your tiredness. What were the causes of this problem and how did you solve it?

2. Choose one of these quotations and write an essay explaining what the quote means, whether you agree with it or not, and why you chose it. In these quotes, a "dream" has a meaning different from REM sleep. What other meaning does a "dream" have here?

> "Throw your dreams into space like a kite,
> and you do not know what they will bring back: a new life,
> a new friend, a new love, a new country."
>
> (Anais Nin, 20th-century writer)

> "The future belongs to those who believe in the beauty of their dreams."
>
> (Eleanor Roosevelt, wife of former president
> Franklin Delano Roosevelt)

> "Reality is wrong. Dreams are for real."
>
> (Tupac Shakur, 20th-century rapper)

3. The **surrealists** were artists at the start of the 20th century who made visual art or poetry with a dream-like atmosphere.

Look at the picture below by Marc Chagall, which illustrates dreams. Then in your notebook, write descriptions of your own dreams. What would your dreams look like if they were drawn or painted as art? You might want to include a drawing or painting of your own along with your description.

UNIT 7 HOW I'LL BECOME AN AMERICAN

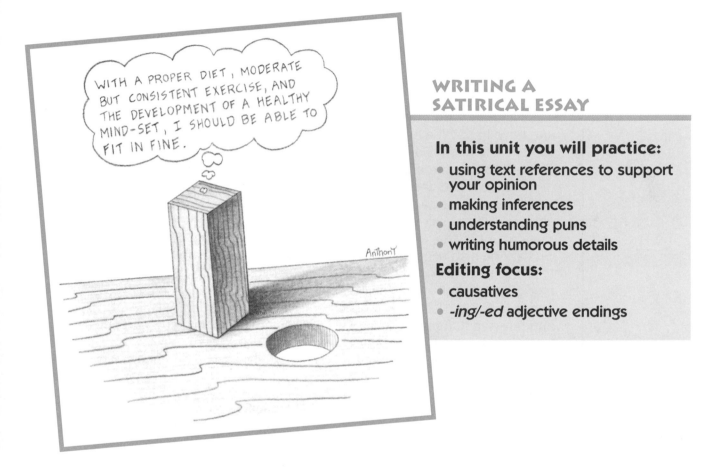

WRITING A SATIRICAL ESSAY

In this unit you will practice:
- using text references to support your opinion
- making inferences
- understanding puns
- writing humorous details

Editing focus:
- causatives
- *-ing/-ed* adjective endings

 Fluency Practice: Speaking and Freewriting

What kinds of jokes are popular in your language? Are they similar to any jokes you have heard in English? Choose your favorite joke from your own language. Translate it into English and tell it to a partner. Did your partner understand the joke? Was it funnier in English or in your native language?

Write for ten minutes in response to these questions and the above activity. Try to express yourself as well as you can. Don't worry about mistakes. Share your writing with a partner.

Miklós Vámos (1951–present) is a Hungarian novelist and playwright. Vámos wrote this essay for *The New York Times* when he was spending a year at the Yale School of Drama in New Haven, Connecticut.

HOW I'LL BECOME AN AMERICAN
by Miklós Vámos

I have been Hungarian for 38 years. I'll try something else for the next 38. I'll try to be an American, for instance. North American, I mean. As an American, I'll speak English fluently. I'll make American mistakes instead of Hungarian mistakes and I'll call them slang.

5 As an American, I'll have a credit card. Or two. I'll use and misuse them and have to pay the fees. I'll apply for other cards right away. Golden Visa. Golden American. Golden Gate. And I'll buy a car, a great American car. Then I'll sell my car and buy a smaller West German car because it's more reliable and doesn't use so much gasoline. Later, I'll sell it and buy a 10 smaller Japanese car with a computer aboard. Then I'll sell it and buy a camper. When I sell the camper, I'll buy a bicycle.

As an American, I'll buy a dog. And a cat. And a goat. And a white whale. And also some big stones as pets.

I'll live in my own house. It will be mine, except for the 99 percent 15 mortgage.[1] I'll sell my house and buy a condo.[2] I'll sell my condo and buy a mobile home. I'll sell my mobile home and buy an igloo.[3] I'll sell my igloo and buy a tent. As an American, I'll be clever: I'll sell my igloo and buy a tent when I move to Florida from Alaska.

Anyway, I'll move a lot. And I'll buy the best dishwasher, microwave, 20 dryer, and hi-fi in the world—that is, the U.S.A. I'll have a warranty for all— or my money back. I'll use automatic toothbrushes, egg boilers, and garage doors. I'll call every single phone number starting 1-800.

I'll buy the fastest food I can get and I'll eat it very slowly because I'll watch TV during the meals. Of course, I'll buy a VCR. I'll watch the taped 25 programs and then retape. Sometimes I'll retape first.

As an American, I'll have an answering machine, too. The outgoing message will promise that I'll call you back as soon as possible, but it won't be possible soon.

If I answer the phone as an exception, I'll tell you that I can't talk now 30 because I have a long-distance call on the other line, but I'll call you back as soon as possible (see above).

And I'll get a job. I'll always be looking for a better job, but I won't get the job I want. I'll work really hard since as an American I wanna[4] be rich.

---

1. *mortgage:* bank loan to buy a house or apartment
2. *condo:* condominium; apartment
3. *igloo:* ice house built by Inuits (Eskimos), who live in the Arctic
4. *wanna:* want to

I'll always be in a hurry: Time is Money. Unfortunately, my time won't be
35 worth as much money as my bosses' time. Sometimes I will have some
time and I still won't have enough money. Then I'll start to hate the
wisdom of this saying.

As an American, sometimes I'll be badly depressed. I'll be the patient of
12 psychiatrists, and I'll be disappointed with all of them. I'll try to change
40 my life a little bit. I'll try to exchange my wives, my cars, my lovers, my
houses, my children, my jobs, my pets.

Sometimes I'll exchange a few dollars into other currencies and I'll
travel to Europe, Hawaii, Tunisia, Martinique, and Japan. I'll be happy to
see that people all over the world are jealous of us Americans. I'll take at
45 least 2,000 snapshots on each trip. I'll also buy a video camera and shoot
everywhere. I'll look at the tapes, photos, and slides, and I'll try to
remember my experiences when I have time or I am in the mood because
I get depressed again and again.

I'll smoke cigarettes. Then I'll be afraid of cancer and I'll stop. I'll smoke
50 cigars. I'll take a breather. I'll try to stop but I won't be able to. I'll call
1-800-222-HELP. If nothing helps and I am still unhappy, I'll make a final
effort. I'll try to read a book. I'll buy some bestsellers. I'll prefer James A.
Michener. My second favorite will be *How to Be Rich in Seven Weeks*. I'll
try to follow this advice in seven years.

55 I'll always be concerned about my health as an American. I won't eat
anything but health food until I get ill. From time to time, I'll read in the
paper that I should stop eating meat, sugar, bread, fiber, grains, iron,
toothpaste, and that I should stop drinking milk, soda, water, acid rain.[5]
I'll try to follow this advice, but then I'll read in the paper that I should do it
60 the other way around.

I'll be puzzled. "Hey, I don't even know what cholesterol[6] is!" Yet I'll stick
to decaf coffee, sugar-free cookies, salt-free butter, and lead-free
gasoline. I'll believe that proper diet and exercise make life longer. I'll go
jogging every day until I am mugged[7] twice and knocked down three
65 times. Then I'll just exercise in my room, but it will also increase my
appetite. I'll go on several diets, and little by little I'll reach 200 pounds.

As an American, I'll buy a new TV every time a larger screen appears
on the market. In the end, the screen will be larger than the room. It will
be difficult to put this enormous TV into my living room; thus, I will put my
70 living room into the TV. Anyway, my living room will look very much like the
living rooms you can see in the soaps:[8] nobody will complain. I won't
complain either. I'll always smile. After all, we are Americans, aren't we?

---

5. *acid rain:* rain polluted by chemicals from industry
6. *cholesterol:* fatty deposits in the blood
7. *mugged:* attacked and robbed in a public place
8. *soaps:* soap operas; daytime radio or television serial dramas

A. General Understanding

1. Identifying Main Topics

Put a check (✓) next to the main topics that Miklós Vámos writes about in "How I'll Become an American." Then in your notebook, write the other topics Vámos mentions.

_____ Music	_____ Art appreciation	_____ Health
_____ Crime	_____ The environment	_____ Money

2. Discussing Main Ideas

Working with a partner, read these statements based upon the Vámos reading. First, in your own words write why each statement is true. Then support the statement by quoting an example from the reading. Write the example and its line numbers on the lines provided.

1. Buying things with cash is not what Americans normally do.

   Line numbers: _14–15_

   Example: Americans buy everything on credit, including their homes. Vámos writes, "I'll live in my own house. It will be mine, except for the 99 percent mortgage."

2. Americans think the best things in the world are found only in America.

   Line numbers: _____

   Example: _____

   _____

3. Change is a constant in American life.

   Line numbers: _____

   Example: _____

   _____

4. Americans love to have a choice.

   Line numbers: _____

   Example: _____

   _____

5. Americans are very materialistic.

   Line numbers: _____

   Example: _____

   _____

6. Americans think time is valuable.

   Line numbers: _____

   Example: _____

   _____

7. Americans are too easily influenced by the media.

   Line numbers: _____

   Example: _____

   _____

3. Reading Between the Lines

Write your responses to these questions about the Vámos reading. Use your own words. Then share what you have written with a partner.

1. Miklós Vámos makes fun of Americans, but do you think he likes them? Why or why not?

   _____

   _____

2. Vámos says he wants to be an American, yet he is very critical of America. Do you think that a person can criticize a country and still want to live there?

   _____

   _____

3. To make his writing humorous, Vámos exaggerates certain characteristics of American life. How do you think the majority of Americans would react to Vámos's description of America and Americans?

   _____

   _____

B. Working with Language

1. Satire: The Language of Humor

Vámos's essay is a **satire** of American values. A **satire** is a piece of writing or work of art, often political, that makes fun of a subject in order to criticize it. The following techniques are used in satire to create humor:

Putting opposites together: placing two contradictory ideas or words near each other.

> "I'll **buy** a car. Then I'll **sell** my car."

> "I'll have a credit card. Or two. I'll **use** and **misuse** them."

Exaggerating: making something seem larger, better, worse, etc., than it really is.

> "As an American, I'll buy a new TV **every time** a larger screen appears on the market. In the end, the screen will be **larger than the room.**"

Using repetition: repeating the same word or phrases for comic effect.

> "*Golden* Visa. *Golden* American. *Golden* Gate."

The example above repeats *golden* to make fun of American materialism.

Ending with an unexpected surprise: ending a sentence or paragraph with a situation opposite from what is expected, or substituting one word for another for a surprise effect.

> "I'll buy a car, **a great American car.** Then I'll sell my car and buy a smaller West German car because it's more reliable and doesn't use so much gasoline. Later, I'll sell it and buy a smaller Japanese car with a computer aboard. Then I'll sell it and buy a camper. When I sell the camper, I'll buy **a bicycle.**"

Read these excerpts from the Vámos reading and write a sentence explaining the humorous techniques he used from those listed above. Then in your notebook, copy a different paragraph from the Vámos reading and explain the humorous techniques used. Compare your answers with a partner's.

1. "I have been Hungarian for 38 years. I'll try something else for the next 38. I'll try to be an American, for instance. North American, I mean. As an American, I'll speak English fluently. I'll make American mistakes instead of Hungarian mistakes, and I'll call them slang."

_____

_____

_____

2. "I'll buy the fastest food I can get and I'll eat it very slowly because I'll watch TV during the meals. Of course, I'll buy a VCR. I'll watch the taped programs and then retape. Sometimes I'll retape first."

_____

_____

_____

_____

3. "I'll always be concerned about my health as an American. I won't eat anything but health food until I get ill. From time to time, I'll read in the paper that I should stop eating meat, sugar, bread, fiber, grains, iron, toothpaste, and that I should stop drinking milk, soda, water, acid rain. I'll try to follow this advice, but then I'll read in the paper that I should do it the other way around."

_____

_____

_____

_____

4. "I'll be puzzled. 'Hey, I don't even know what cholesterol is!' Yet I'll stick to decaf coffee, sugar-free cookies, salt-free butter, and lead-free gasoline. I'll believe that proper diet and exercise make life longer. I'll go jogging every day until I am mugged twice and knocked down three times. Then I'll just exercise in my room, but it will also increase my appetite. I'll go on several diets, and little by little I'll reach 200 pounds."

_____

_____

_____

_____

III ▷ Prewriting Activities

A. Puns

1. Understanding Puns

A **pun** is the use of one word that has two or more meanings or the use of two words with a similar sound but different meanings. A pun is used for comic effect and appears in writing and satirical cartoons.

Bakers never have time to **loaf** off.

The above sentence is a pun because *loaf* has two meanings—as a noun it means baked bread and as a verb it means to be lazy.

I'll buy the **fastest food** I can get and eat it very slowly.

The above sentence is a pun because the adverb *fastest* is a play on the noun *fast food*.

Study the cartoon below. Then discuss with a partner how it illustrates a pun.

"Being a stockbroker isn't easy, son. Wall Street is a rat race!"

2. Identifying Puns

Read these excerpts from an actual student composition called "How an American Will Become a Taiwanese." In your notebook, explain the puns the student writer used.

1. "Many Taiwanese and Americans do not at first like each other's food. Americans can't stomach Taiwanese specialty dishes such as bear claws and animal brains. Taiwanese, on the other hand, dislike some American dishes such as Southern fried chicken, which the Taiwanese think has a **fowl** taste."

   The word "fowl," which means chicken, is a pun on the word "foul," which means bad or unpleasant.

2. "A Taiwanese would not use a fork or knife because such sharp utensils are thought to be unlucky. They **cut into** the smooth communication that we try to achieve with each other."

3. "Most Taiwanese like high tech and they admire people in Silicon Valley who live in the **laptop of luxury**."

4. "Everything about Western popular music **strikes a chord** among Taiwanese young people."

5. "Because we are afraid of inflation, we value gold more than money. When a poor Taiwanese becomes rich, instead of moving to a mansion, he stays in a house that looks like it is about to fall apart. However, because he doesn't move to a mansion, he is able to save a huge pile of gold, which he keeps locked in a safe inside his house. The house may not look like much from the outside, but you can be sure it's **worth its weight in gold**."

B. Open for Discussion

Read these sayings about humor. In a small group, discuss what you think they mean and whether you agree or disagree with them. Take notes and write a summary of your group's discussion.

1. "Laugh, and the whole world laughs with you. Weep, and you weep alone."
2. "A good way to cope with life's difficulties is through humor."
3. "You cannot possibly be a serious person if you don't know how to laugh."
4. "Laughter is the best medicine."

IV Structured Writing Focus

YOUR TASK

Write a five-paragraph satirical essay telling how an American can become a member of another culture that you know well. Use humor to write about any three of the following topics: interpersonal communication, consumerism, crime, the environment, food, health, media, money, politics, technology, or work.

ALTERNATIVE TASK: **Write a five-paragraph satirical essay. Use humor to explain what a person from another city or neighborhood could do to fit into the city or neighborhood where you live.**

A. Starting to Write

1. Before You Brainstorm

Read this essay written by a Japanese student and answer the questions that follow. Compare your answers with those of your classmates and teacher.

STUDENT ESSAY FIRST DRAFT

Dear American Who Wants to Be Japanese

There are three secrets to becoming Japanese. They will not be hard to communicate. The really hard part is living with these secrets.

First of all, you should speak awkward Japanese with a heavy American accent and keep your blond hair. If you don't have blond hair, you should dye it because most Japanese expect Americans to be blond. Your American appearance will help you to fit in with the Japanese, who like Americans and who still believe America is a place where wealthy people live and enjoy an advanced culture. They also think that it is the best country in the world. Even though the Japanese are beginning to realize that America is not an ideal country, their belief that America is great has not changed much. So as long as you have a foreign look, many Japanese people will treat you very well as a guest from the number-one country.

Second, you should do everything completely opposite from the way you did it in America. In America, you bought a large car and kept changing to smaller cars or a bicycle. In Japan, you should start with a bicycle and end up with a large car. To have a large car, you will need to look for a parking space, which will cost almost as much as your apartment rent and which will be far from your apartment. (Maybe you can keep your bicycle to go to your parking space!) In America, you had a house first and then kept moving to a smaller home, such as an apartment or a tent. In Japan, you can't live in a tent because there is no free space for camping and no one will allow you to live in his or her garden. Instead, you should start with an apartment. You will end up with a small house from which you will have a two-hour commute to work in a crowded train. This commute will also deplete almost all your salary for the next 30 years!

Third, you have to be aware of the things you should not do. Do not change your job because you will have to borrow money from the bank to keep paying for your house. If you change your job, everything will start over. You will have a small apartment and a bicycle.

Now you are on your way to becoming Japanese. Enjoy your new life, which is guaranteed to be nothing special. It is what we Japanese call "peace."

1. Does the introduction give background information on Japanese culture to show how it is different from American culture?

2. Is the thesis statement clear?

3. Does each body paragraph give enough examples to support the main idea of that paragraph? If not, where should more examples be added?

4. Does the conclusion refer to the thesis statement?

5. Do you have any comments to add?

Now read the second draft of the student essay and answer the questions that follow it. Compare your answers with those of your classmates and teacher.

Dear American Who Wants to Be Japanese

No two nationalities are alike, and the differences between Japanese and Americans are great. We Japanese belong to an ancient culture. You Americans live together in a relatively new society made up of people from all over the world. Your population of 280 million people shares a large area of land, while our population of 127 million is crammed into the limited space of our small island. This lack of space has forced us to cooperate with each other throughout the years in order to survive. Instead of becoming individualists like you, we have been taught to obey many rules in order to live in harmony with each other. In order to become Japanese, you will have to learn these three secrets: don't hide your American appearance, do everything opposite from the way you did it in America, and be aware of what is forbidden.

First of all, because we like American culture, you should keep your American appearance. For instance, you should speak awkward Japanese with a heavy American accent and keep your blond hair. If you don't have blond hair already, you should dye it because most Japanese expect Americans to be blond. Your American appearance will help you to fit in with the Japanese, who like Americans and who still believe that America is a place where wealthy people enjoy an advanced culture. They also think that it is the best country in the world. Even though the Japanese are beginning to realize that America is not an ideal country, their belief that America is great has not changed much. So as long as you have a foreign look, many Japanese people will treat you very well as a guest from the number-one country.

Second, you should do everything completely opposite from the way you did it in America. For example, in America, you bought a large car and kept changing to smaller cars or a bicycle. However, in Japan, you should start with a bicycle and end up with a large car. To have a large car, you will need to look for a parking space, which will cost almost as much as your apartment rent and which will be far from your apartment. (Maybe you can keep your bicycle to get to your parking spot!) In America, you had a house and kept moving to a smaller home, such as an apartment or a tent. In Japan, you can't live in a tent because there is no free space for camping and no one will allow you to live in his or her garden. Instead, you should start with an apartment and end up with a small house from which you will have a two-hour commute to work in a crowded train. This commute will also deplete almost all your salary for the next 30 years!

Third, in Japan you have to be aware of things you should not do. There is a long list of "don'ts." Here are a few suggestions regarding your social life and your work life. We Japanese are very modest. To be like us, when you are a host, never tell your guests that you have prepared a wonderful new dish. Instead, say, "I am a terrible cook. I should have thrown the whole dinner away before you came!" As a guest, you should respond with kindness and tell your host that you have never tasted such a delicious meal. Regarding work, you need to remain loyal to your boss because if you have to change your job, you will lose your comfortable lifestyle. You will have to get a bigger mortgage from the bank, and you will go into debt. If you change your job, everything will start over. You will have a small apartment and a bicycle.

Once you learn the "dos and don'ts" of being Japanese, you will be well on your way to joining our society. It will not be an easy thing for you to do. Frankly, it is easier to talk about these "secrets" than it is to live with them. Nevertheless, if you have patience and make every effort to become one of us and obey our rules, you will start to enjoy your new life here because you will live in harmony with everyone else on our small island. We Japanese call this "peace."

1. Compare the introductions in the first and second drafts. Why is the introduction of the second draft more effective?

2. How has the thesis statement changed in the second draft?

3. What support has been added to the third body paragraph?

4. Underline the transitional expressions used in the essay, (*for example, for instance, first, second, third, instead,* etc.)

5. Compare the conclusions of the first and second drafts. Why is the conclusion of the second draft more effective?

6. Do you have any other comments on this essay? Do you see any other improvements in the second draft?

2. Brainstorming

Look at the Structured Writing Focus on page 128 for some suggested topics for your satirical essay. Choose three of them and write notes in your notebook on the differences between American culture and another culture as they relate to those topics. Use the style below as a model.

Your title: "How an American Will Become _____"

Topic: _____

American Culture

_____ (another culture)

_____ _____

_____ _____

_____ _____

_____ _____

Write notes in your notebook describing your city or neighborhood and its residents. Explain how a foreigner can fit in.

Example essay titles:
"An Out-of-Towner Comes to the City of Angels (Los Angeles)"
"My Neighborhood—How to Fit In"
"Living in the Suburbs"

B. Preparing the First Draft

1. Creating Humorous Details

Reread the second draft of the student essay on pages 130–131. Write on the lines below what makes the essay funny. Then discuss your response with a partner.

_____

_____

_____

_____

Read the humorous details below taken from student essays. Then write your own humorous details in your notebook, using your brainstorming notes. You may use puns, opposites, exaggeration, unexpected surprise, repetition, or other techniques. When you have finished, share your writing with a partner.

HUMOROUS DETAILS

Describing his countrymen's obsession with safety, a Swedish student writes:

"My fellow Swedes would be happy if they could drive their cars wearing helmets and space suits."

Laughing at his fellow citizens' passion for maps, a French student writes:

"With their eyes glued to the details of a map, many French men and women are run over while walking toward an address on the other side of the street."

---

2. Organizing Your Essay

Study this block diagram of a five-paragraph essay to plan a first draft of your essay. In your notebook, draw your own diagram and write your notes in each of its sections.

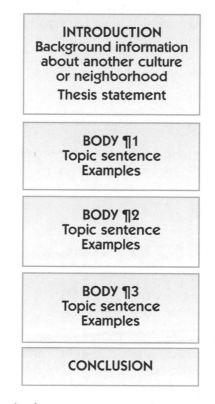

INTRODUCTION
Background information about another culture or neighborhood
Thesis statement

BODY ¶1
Topic sentence
Examples

BODY ¶2
Topic sentence
Examples

BODY ¶3
Topic sentence
Examples

CONCLUSION

*Write a **first draft** of your essay. Remember to write in complete sentences and try to use some of the vocabulary and structures that you have practiced in this unit.*

C. Revising the First Draft

When you have finished writing your first draft, read it to a partner.

CHECKLIST FOR REVISING THE FIRST DRAFT

When you listen to your partner's essay and when you discuss your own, keep these questions in mind:

1. **Does the thesis statement prepare the reader for the topics in the body paragraphs?**

2. **Does each body paragraph discuss a different topic?**

3. **Does the writer clearly describe his or her culture or neighborhood?**

4. **Does the writer use transitional expressions (*for example, for instance, first, second,* etc.) to introduce examples?**

5. **Does the writer use humorous techniques such as puns?**

After discussing your essay with a partner, some reorganization may be necessary. You may also have to consider communicating some of your ideas in a different way.

*Now write a **second draft** that includes all of your additions and changes.*

D. Editing the Second Draft

After you have written a second draft, proofread your work for any errors and correct them. These guidelines and exercises should help.

1. Causatives

When we persuade, force, allow, or encourage someone to do something, we use a **causative** construction:

She **had** the plumber **fix** the water.
She will **get** her son **to wash** the car.

In the above sentences "To **have** someone **do** something" implies that you hire someone to do a job. "To **get** someone to **do** something" implies that you convince someone to do something.

verb + object + base form	verb + object + infinitive
let someone **do** something	**encourage** someone **to do** something
make someone **do** something	**get** someone **to do** something
have someone **do** something	**persuade/convince** someone **to do** something
	force someone **to do** something

Working with a partner, find the mistakes in this student composition. Examine the words in bold print. If there is an error, correct it with a causative construction. If there is no error, put a check (✓) above it. There are five more mistakes.

to become
Colombian parents encourage their children ~~become~~ good, honest citizens. They do this by getting them **to learn** everything about their ancestors. Although children can learn a lot at home about their culture and ancestors without receiving a formal education, Colombian parents are convinced that if they make their children **studying** hard at school, their children will enter a university and find a good job.

However, Colombian parents realize that studying isn't everything: without good health, nothing else matters. That is why Colombian parents have their children **eat** all-natural foods. They don't let their children **to consume** too many unhealthy snacks or too much fast food. They prepare three nutritious meals a day. Some Colombians make their friends **to feeling** ashamed when their friends confess to eating "American food" such as hamburgers and hot-dogs.

Even though Colombians care about their health, when Colombians become ill, they don't go to the doctor. Colombians consider being ill a sign of weakness. Instead, they persuade people **to believe** that they are staying home for another reason. They make themselves **to feel** better, instead of going to the doctor. Then they only leave the house when they have got all of the symptoms **disappeared**.

2. *-ing/-ed* Adjective Endings

Two common endings for adjectives are *-ing* and *-ed.* Both adjective endings describe emotions.

-ing refers to the person or thing *causing* an emotion

-ed refers to the person *feeling* the emotion

Our history teacher is **inspiring.** We enjoy her lectures on medieval history.
Our history teacher is **inspired.** She loves to talk about about medieval history.

The **exciting** cook is fun to watch as he prepares chicken with teriyaki sauce.
The **excited** cook keeps talking about what interests him most: food.

Working with a partner, look at this map of the Republic of Georgia. Complete the paragraphs, with the correct form of the adjectives in parentheses.

Americans are __inspired__ *(inspiring / inspired)* by the hospitality of

Georgians. When an American stays as a guest in a Georgian's house, he is

_____ *(overwhelming / overwhelmed)* by all the attention his hosts give

him. Another _____ *(surprising / surprised)* observation that

Americans often make about Georgians is the respect that they show to old

men and old women. Georgians always give their seats to elderly people

on the bus and never put their elderly relatives in retirement homes.

Many Americans are also _____ *(amazing / amazed)* by the
Georgians' reverence and love for mothers. In the Georgian language,
"motherland" is the word for native country, the capital city is the "mother
city," and the earth is "the motherland." Another characteristic of
Georgians is their attachment to their homeland. Because all Georgians are
_____ *(nurturing / nurtured)* with a great love for their country, they
don't like to leave it for too long. They are not that _____ *(interesting /
interested)* in the _____ *(fascinating / fascinated)* customs of others.
"Home, sweet home" is the Georgians' motto.

E. Preparing the Final Draft

*Reread your second draft and correct any errors you find. Put a check (✓) in each
space as you edit for these points. Then write your corrected final version.*

> **CHECKLIST FOR EDITING THE SECOND DRAFT**
> _____ **causatives**
> _____ ***-ing/-ed* adjective endings**

Additional Writing Opportunities

Write about one of the following topics.

1. Many films and TV programs focus on a particular aspect of people's behavior or relationships. Choose your favorite comedy (film or TV program). Describe why you think topics or characters in the film or show are funny and explain what the film or show tells you about society or human nature. Use examples by referring to specific scenes or characters, or to the story itself.

2. For some people, keeping a sense of humor during a crisis is often the best way to deal with a difficult situation. Has this been true for you? for someone you know? for a famous person you can think of? Write an essay about how humor can be used to survive a crisis. Give examples of specific cases where people used humor to cope with their problems.

3. Choose one of the following quotes, which you discussed in class. Write an essay explaining the meaning of the quote and whether you agree or disagree with it. Include some examples from books that you have read or from real life to support your opinion.

    "Laugh, and the whole world laughs with you.
      Weep, and you weep alone."

    "You cannot possibly be a serious person
      if you don't know how to laugh."

    "Laughter is the best medicine."

8 FOR AND AGAINST BILINGUAL EDUCATION

WRITING AN ARGUMENTATIVE ESSAY

In this unit you will practice:

- defending your point of view
- refuting opposing views
- conceding to an opposing view and replying
- using the language of concession

Editing focus:

- present unreal conditionals
- connectors: *despite / despite the fact that* and *although / even though*

I Fluency Practice: Freewriting

When people move to a new country, should they completely assimilate into the culture of that new country or should they keep some aspects of the culture of their old country? Which aspects would be most important for them to keep? their food? clothing? music? entertainment? work habits? religion? language?

Write for ten minutes. Try to express yourself as well as you can. Don't worry about mistakes. Share your writing with a partner.

II ▸ Reading for Writing

In recent years there has been a debate over whether U.S. public schools should use **English as a second language (ESL) programs** or **bilingual education programs** to teach English to students who are not proficient in it. ESL programs are taught entirely in English, but the English language is simplified and explained. Bilingual education programs teach in the students' native language and also teach English as one of their subjects. Bilingual education was started in part because many children could not read or write in their native language, and it was thought that they would be able to learn English more easily if they became literate in their native language first. The article below explores the views of some parents living in New York City, who argue for and against bilingual education.

BILINGUAL EDUCATION: PARENTS' VIEWS

Yuliya Kovardinskaya remembers being thrown into an 11th-grade classroom when she arrived from Ukraine ten years ago and not understanding much of what she was taught. In this sink-or-swim[1] environment, she swam. By 12th grade, she had moved from an ESL
5 program to a regular classroom. So when she sent her five-year-old son to school last September, she refused a bilingual program, in which teaching is done mostly in the native language, in favor of ESL classes, where the instruction is in English. "You have to be with people who speak English to speak the language," Ms. Kovardinskaya, 25, said.

10 Yet Sandra Almanzar had a different experience as a schoolgirl and chose a different path for her daughter. When Ms. Almanzar came from the Dominican
15 Republic, she said, she thrived[2] in a bilingual program and moved within a year to regular classes. Ms. Almanzar, 32, has enrolled her six-year-old daughter in a dual
20 language program where subjects are taught in English one day and in Spanish the next. "I go back and forth to my country, and I want her to be able to communicate with my
25 family," she said.

Sandra Almanzar with her daughter, Adriana Arias

---

1. *sink or swim:* to be in a situation where one will fail or survive based on one's own efforts
2. *thrive:* to succeed

Sometimes, the degree to which parents want their children to assimilate is determined by family dynamics. Yvonia Direny, 33, a native of Haiti whose ten-year-old son and seven-year-old daughter attend bilingual programs in Creole, said that for her family Creole was a necessity. Their
30 father, who speaks mostly Creole, can help them with their homework. Their Creole-speaking grandmother can baby-sit. Also for Elizabeth Cabrera, 38, "The important thing is that they don't forget Spanish." She said the schools would teach her children "correct" Spanish much better than she could ever do herself. "The more languages they know, the more
35 opportunities they'll have," she said.

On the other end, there are parents who expect the schools to put their children quickly on an equal footing[3] with American students by immersing[4] them in English. Among these is Romana Khan, a homemaker who arrived in New York eight years ago from Pakistan with her husband,
40 a cabdriver, and who speaks Urdu to her four children. She said she wants her children to be bilingual, but not in school. "New York is the city of immigrants, and most of them speak their native languages at home," said Ms. Khan. "So when we send them to school we just say, 'Please teach English to them.'"

45 Ms. Situ Fyang, 45, said that she stood solidly behind bilingual education because of her children's older age. She said that when she enrolled her twin sons, now 16, in school after arriving from China three years ago, she worried that they would drop out[5] because of the culture shock. The bilingual program, she said, has given the boys time to adjust
50 to their new life. She argued that for teenage children, unlike elementary school children, it is easier to keep up with subjects in their native language and later catch up on their English. Students in New York City have to pass city and state exams to pass on to the next grade, and except for the English tests, city and state exams are offered in native
55 languages. "If we had put them in an English class, they would have been lost," Ms. Fyang said through a translator.

But in some school districts, parents have rejected bilingual programs en masse.[6] In District 21 in Brooklyn, Russian immigrants have historically opted for ESL programs instead of bilingual classes, said Anita Malta,
60 executive assistant to the superintendent.

"We would form a class, and they'd say no," she said. "They were concerned about bilingual education holding their kids back."

3. *to be on an equal footing:* to have equal status and equal opportunities
4. *immersing them in English:* putting them in an environment where only English is used
5. *drop out:* leave school without graduating
6. *en masse:* as a whole

A. General Understanding

Write answers in your notebook to these questions about the reading on pages 140–141. Then compare your answers with a partner's.

1. What are the differences between ESL programs and bilingual education programs?

2. Why did some parents not want bilingual education programs for their children?

3. Why did some parents say that it was important for teenagers to have bilingual education classes instead of ESL classes?

4. Why did some parents want their children to speak the language of their country of origin even though their children were born in the United States?

B. Working with Language

Match the underlined words in the sentences with their synonyms in this list. Write your answers in your notebook and compare them with a partner's.

adjust to	**expected to**	**refused**
catch up with	**educated**	**stood solidly behind**
concerned	**on an equal footing**	**supportive**
declined	**proficient**	**thrived**

1. Many immigrants who came to the United States in the past faced difficulties before they could <u>adapt to</u> American life and feel comfortable here.

2. Among the first immigrants to the United States were the English, who <u>succeeded</u> in their new home starting in 17th century. Many of them came to find religious freedom in the New World.

3. The Irish came to the United States to escape from starvation during the "Great Hunger" in Ireland (1845–1848). They were very poor, but many were <u>competent</u> in English. Their knowledge of the language helped them succeed.

4. Germans were one of the largest immigrant groups to come to the United States. Many came because political freedom had <u>decreased</u> in Germany after the failed Democratic Revolution of 1848.

5. Many Scandinavians heard about the Great Plains in the New World, and they <u>thought they would</u> find good farmland when they came to the United States in the 19th century. They were not disappointed.

6. Chinese laborers, who came to work in the gold mines of California and stayed to build the railroads, were the only immigrant group <u>denied</u> further entry into the United States in the 1880s as a result of discrimination and prejudice.

7. The workers who built the New York City subways were not all paid <u>the same</u>: the employment signs often promised more money to Irish workers because they were native speakers of English.

8. Immigrants did not always feel accepted by other Americans. They often grouped together in neighborhoods where they could create a more understanding and <u>helpful</u> community.

9. Most immigrants <u>supported</u> education because they believed it would lead to material success for their children and for themselves. Even so, it often took immigrants several generations before they could <u>reach</u> the level of prosperity of other Americans.

10. In early U.S. history, English was not the only language in which students were <u>instructed</u>: in Louisiana they were taught in French, and elsewhere in the country some students were taught in German, Dutch, Greek, and Swedish. Since World War I, however, public schools have taught subjects in English.

11. Immigration was limited by the U.S. government after World War I and remained at minimum levels for almost 50 years. When mass immigration was permitted again in the 1960s, Americans were <u>worried</u> about how difficult assimilation would be for the new immigrants, mainly from South America and Asia. That is why most Americans at that time agreed to bilingual education programs.

Prewriting Activities

A. Categorizing Arguments For and Against Bilingual Education

1. Identifying Arguments

Read these statements from parents. Next to each statement, write "F" if the statement is for bilingual education, or "A" if the statement is against bilingual education. Then in your notebook, write additional arguments for or against bilingual education.

_____ 1. "Teach in the child's native language to protect his or her native language, culture, and heritage."

_____ 2. "The more languages children know, the more opportunities they will have."

_____ 3. "If students with limited English are always separated from native speakers, they will have a hard time learning English. Practice makes perfect."

_____ 4. "I want my children to speak English in their classes so that they will learn it well and can become doctors and lawyers."

_____ 5. "Older students would be lost without bilingual programs, which help them get better scores in math and science."

_____ 6. "My family has to take care of my children while I am at work. My children must be able to speak my family's language."

_____ 7. "Bilingual education is a costly bureaucracy that exists at the taxpayer's expense."

_____ 8. "Children whose families don't speak English at home must learn English in the primary grades to get enough exposure to the language."

_____ 9. "Bilingual education has made it possible for parents who don't speak English to participate in their children's education."

_____ 10. "Bilingual education is harmful to our society because it divides and separates non-native speakers from native speakers."

_____ 11. "My children have the best chance of passing their high school exit exams if they study their subjects in our language. I want my children to graduate so they can earn a better living."

_____ 12. "I want my children to be a full part of our new country and culture, so they should study their subjects in English."

2. Categorizing Arguments

Categorize the parents' statements from the previous exercise. Decide if each one is a cultural, economic, or educational argument and whether it is for or against bilingual education. Write the number for each statement under the appropriate category below. When you have finished, compare your answers with a partner's.

	Cultural Arguments	Economic Arguments	Educational Arguments
For bilingual education	1		
Against bilingual education			

B. Open for Discussion

Take notes as your group discusses the questions below. Then as a group, write a summary of the most interesting parts of your discussion. Share your group's summary with a classmate who was not part of your group.

1. Do you speak one language at home and another at school? If so, has this been a problem for you? Do you use different languages in different situations?

2. If English were made the official language of the United States, signs and official documents would be in English only and would not be translated into other languages as they are now. Would you be in favor of this?

3. Why does the United States accept so many immigrants? How do immigrants contribute to this country?

4. Did your family immigrate to the United States? If so, how long ago was that? What kinds of difficulties did you or your family experience in adjusting to life in a new place?

IV Structured Writing Focus

Write a five-paragraph argumentative essay for or against bilingual education.

ALTERNATIVE TASK: Is immigrating to another country a good way to improve one's life? Write a five-paragraph argumentative essay on this topic.

A. Starting to Write

1. Brainstorming

FOR THE MAIN TASK

Consider all of the arguments you have read both for and against bilingual education. In your notebook, write down the arguments that impressed you the most. Add your own ideas. Be honest and express your feelings. Then consider these questions for your thesis statement:

Do you tend to agree or disagree with bilingual education?

Which side would you prefer to write about?

Do you have any personal experience with bilingual education?

FOR THE ALTERNATIVE TASK

In your notebook, write all of your ideas about why people immigrate to another country. Then consider these questions for your thesis statement:

What are some of the reasons that people decide to emigrate (leave their native country)?

What are the difficulties that immigrants face when they leave their old country? when they come to a new country?

What are the advantages of experiencing and living in two cultures?

Do you have a personal experience with immigration in your family? Have you read any books that could help you explain your feelings?

2. Thesis Statements for Argumentative Essays

The aim of an argumentative essay is to convince readers to agree with your position. Your thesis statement must show a clear point of view with three reasons that you will argue in the body of your essay. Remember, a thesis statement cannot be a mere statement of fact. For example, you cannot simply give information about bilingual education or immigration, you must state your *opinion*.

THESIS STATEMENT FOR AN ARGUMENTATIVE ESSAY

Bilingual education would be a fine idea if there were more parental choice, more qualified teachers who also speak English, and a strict limit of two years in bilingual classes for students.

This is a good thesis statement because it takes a clear position: bilingual education is good, but some changes must be made to the programs. The thesis statement also establishes three supporting arguments for the body paragraphs: parental choice, more qualified teachers, and bilingual classes limited to two years.

Put a check (✓) next to each statement that would make a good thesis statement for a five-paragraph argumentative essay. If it is a good thesis statement, write the arguments of the three body paragraphs that would follow it. If it is not a good thesis statement, explain why.

_____ 1. Bilingual education should be stopped because its programs discriminate against immigrants.

> This is not a good thesis statement. It is a clear statement of opinion, but it does not give arguments to defend that opinion in the body paragraphs.

_____ 2. In this essay I will explain why I agree with bilingual education.

_____

_____

_____

_____ 3. Immigrants need specialized services, a great deal of exposure to the English language, and time to adjust to American customs. In my opinion, bilingual education offers none of these things.

_____

_____

_____

_____ 4. Bilingual education has its good and bad points.

_____

_____

_____

_____ 5. English should be the only language for people in the United States because one language will make us one people— economically, culturally, and educationally.

_____

_____

_____

_____ 6. Parents, not school administrators, should decide whether their child should attend ESL or bilingual classes. Parents know which one is best for their child and family—psychologically, culturally, and economically.

_____

_____

_____

B. Preparing the First Draft

1. Refutation

An argumentative essay is like a **debate** (a formal public argument or discussion of a question). In order to convince the reader of your point of view, you must show that you know the opposing arguments and can **refute** them (prove that they are incorrect or weak.)

Read this paragraph and complete the tasks below.

PARAGRAPH WITH REFUTATION

Bilingual Education is Good for the U.S. Economy

State the opposite point of view →

Refute the opposition (say why it is incorrect) →

Bilingual education has been unfairly criticized. **Although some people think that bilingual education programs are a waste of taxpayers' money,** it is beyond a question today that immigrant children need bilingual education classes in order to fit into mainstream American life. Many children are not literate in their first language, and it is very hard for them to learn another language. By becoming literate in their first language, children can more easily learn to read and write in English. Some Americans resent the expense of bilingual education because previous generations in their families had to study in regular English classes and did not have the benefit of bilingual education. But the immigrants of the past joined an economy that used more unskilled labor than ours does today. For example, during the Industrial Revolution of the 19th century, it was less important for people to read and write English, whereas our economy now depends more on a literate workforce. It is in the best interest of our country to have a literate population that can do the skilled jobs of the modern world.

In your notebook, write three arguments of your own for or against bilingual education. Then write the opposite point of view for one argument. Write your refutation of that argument. Discuss your choices with a partner.

2. Concession and Reply

You make a **concession** (recognize one good point in the opposition's arguments) to show that you are open-minded and that your point of view stands up to the opposing view. You then **reply** to the opposing argument (discuss its limitations) to prove that your overall point of view is stronger. There should be one **concession** in the third body paragraph of your essay.

Read this paragraph and complete the task below.

PARAGRAPH WITH CONCESSION AND REPLY

Bilingual Education Should End

Bilingual education, although well intended, has failed to meet the needs of children learning English and must be ended. **It is certainly true that immigrant children need specialized services to help them become part of the U.S. economy,** but the specialized services they need are ESL classes, not bilingual classes, to learn English. Although defenders of bilingual education claim that it prepares students for mainstream English classes, bilingual education has instead segregated non-English-speaking children into an academic ghetto. Some students are allowed to stay up to six years in programs where they receive less than one hour a day of instruction in English. Some students rarely interact with native English-speaking children. The result of bilingual education is often academic failure, a high dropout rate, and low self-esteem—problems that the bilingual program was supposed to eliminate. The only way to help immigrant children learn English is to teach them exclusively in ESL classes.

Concession → (points to "It is certainly true...become part of the U.S. economy,")

Reply → (points to "need are ESL classes...teach them exclusively in ESL classes.")

Decide if you are for or against bilingual education. Then choose one argument of the opposing side to concede in your essay. In your notebook, write notes on how you would concede to that argument and what arguments you would use to reply to it. Use the expressions below and discuss your notes with a partner.

THE LANGUAGE OF CONCESSION

The following bolded words can be used to show a concession:

It is true that English has not always been the language of instruction in U.S. schools.

Admittedly, bilingual programs have made it easier for immigrant parents to be more involved in their children's education.

I concede that immigrant children do need specialized services.

I agree that the goal of public education in the United States is to encourage the use of English.

3. Organizing Your Essay

Study this block diagram of a five-paragraph essay to plan a first draft of your essay. In your notebook, draw your own diagram and write your notes in each of its sections.

INTRODUCTION
Background information
Thesis Statement: opinion with 3 arguments

BODY ¶1
Topic sentence
Explanation of point 1
Refutation of opposing point of view

BODY ¶2
Topic sentence
Explanation of point 2
Refutation of opposing point of view

BODY ¶3
Topic sentence
Explanation of point 3
Concession of opposing argument and reply

CONCLUSION
Summary of your 3 points
Discussion of the future outcomes or consequences of the situation

*Write a **first draft** of your essay. Review your notes. This time you must write in complete sentences and paragraphs. It may be helpful to use some of the structures and vocabulary that you have practiced in this unit.*

C. Revising the First Draft

When you have finished writing your first draft, read it to a partner.

CHECKLIST FOR REVISING THE FIRST DRAFT

When you listen to a partner's essay and when you discuss your own, keep these questions in mind:

1. Does the introduction provide the background information necessary to understand the issue?

2. Does the writer state a clear opinion and give three arguments in the thesis?

3. Does each body paragraph develop a different argument and explain it with logic, examples and facts?

4. Are opposing arguments refuted? Is there a concession?

5. Does the conclusion summarize the writer's main arguments and discuss any possible future outcomes or consequences?

After you have discussed your essay with a partner, you may want to reorganize your ideas, omit some, or add new ones.

*Now write a **second draft** that includes all of your additions and changes.*

D. Editing the Second Draft

After you have written a second draft, proofread your work for any errors and correct them. These guidelines and exercises should help.

1. Present Unreal Conditionals

One use of the **present unreal conditional** is to describe a situation that does not exist, but could happen, and the possible consequences of it. (See Unit 4, page 74, for the other use of the present unreal conditional.)

if + simple past + comma + conditional (*would* + base form)

If bilingual education **were** banned throughout the United States**,** immigrant children **would not attend** bilingual classes any more.

When the conditional comes first, the sentence has no comma.

conditional (*would* + base form) + *if* + simple past

Immigrant children **would not attend** bilingual classes anymore **if** bilingual education **were** banned throughout the United States.

Complete each of these sentences with the conditional or simple past form of the verb in parentheses. Compare your answers with a partner's.

1. If bilingual education classes _____ *(make illegal)*, children would have more hours to devote to English.

2. Children _____ *(learn)* English more quickly if they had more instruction in it.

3. If bilingual education _____ *(ban)* throughout the United States, parents could not choose to put their children in bilingual classes.

4. Many bilingual teachers _____ *(lose)* their jobs if all children attended ESL classes.

5. If bilingual education ended, some parents _____ *(be)* unhappy.

2. Connectors

DESPITE AND **DESPITE THE FACT THAT**

Despite and *despite the fact that* contrast two opposite ideas in the same sentence.

Incorrect (no contrast)	Correct (contrasting ideas)
Despite the difficulties, he *failed*.	**Despite** the difficulties, he *succeeded*.

despite + noun or gerund + comma + sentence

<u>**Despite**</u> **the difficulties,** many people still immigrate to the U. S.
          NOUN

<u>**Despite**</u> **struggling** to make a living, many immigrants succeed in the U. S.
          GERUND

despite the fact that + sentence + comma + sentence

<u>**Despite the fact that**</u> **an immigrant's life is difficult,** many people still decide to immigrate.

Change these sentences from one connector form to the other. Compare your answers with a partner's.

1. Despite learning new customs in a new country, most immigrants keep their religion.

   <u>Despite the fact that they learn new customs in a new</u>

   <u>country, most immigrants keep their religion.</u>

2. Despite the fact that they may experience culture shock at first, many immigrants come to love their adopted country.

   <u>Despite experiencing culture shock at first, many immigrants</u>

   <u>come to love their adopted country.</u>

3. Despite immigrants' respect for their native culture, they often come to value cultural aspects of American life.

   _____

   _____

4. Despite the fact that immigrant children may know little English at first, some can learn it very fast.

_____

_____

5. Despite being the main language of the United States, English has never been recognized as the official language.

_____

_____

6. Despite having limited immigration in the past, the United States welcomes immigrants today.

_____

_____

ALTHOUGH AND EVEN THOUGH

Although and *even though* contrast two opposite ideas in the same sentence. The argument appears in the main clause, NOT the subordinate clause. The argument can come before or after the concession.

Argument	**Concession**
We need to pass laws that will make it easier for children to learn English MAIN CLAUSE	**although** some parents will be deprived of their right to choose a bilingual program. SUBORDINATE CLAUSE

Concession	**Argument**
Even though some parents will be deprived of their right to choose a bilingual program, SUBORDINATE CLAUSE	we need to pass laws that will make it easier for children to learn English. MAIN CLAUSE

In the above sentences, the author is FOR banning bilingual education.

Read these arguments for and against bilingual education. Working with a partner, write two sentences in support of one of these points of view using the connectors despite / despite the fact that *or* although / even though. *Make sure to include an argument and concession in each sentence. First study the example answers.*

FOR BILINGUAL EDUCATION	AGAINST BILINGUAL EDUCATION
Knowing more than one language is an advantage in today's world.	English-language proficiency is essential for many careers in the United States.
Immigrant children do better with their school subjects when they are taught in English *and* in their native language.	Immigrant children should be encouraged to speak English in school as soon as possible.
Immigrant children feel lonely at first when they are put in regular classrooms.	Immigrant children should not be separated from other children in school.

FOR BILINGUAL EDUCATION

1. Although knowledge of English is very important on standardized tests, in the business world it can be an advantage to know more than one language.

2. _____

_____

3. _____

_____

AGAINST BILINGUAL EDUCATION

1. Despite the fact that knowing many languages can be helpful later in life, a person cannot succeed in many careers without a thorough and complete knowledge of English.

2. _____

_____

3. _____

_____

E. Preparing the Final Draft

Reread your second draft and correct any errors you find. Put a check (✓) in each space as you edit for these points. Then write your corrected final version.

CHECKLIST FOR EDITING THE SECOND DRAFT

_____ present unreal conditionals

_____ connectors: *despite / despite the fact that* and *although / even though*

V ◆ Additional Writing Opportunities

Write about one of the following topics.

1. Should immigrants assimilate and adopt the culture and customs of their new country, or should they keep the traditions of the country they left? Which aspects of their former culture should they keep? food? clothing? music and entertainment? attitudes toward dating and marriage? religion? language? Write a five-paragraph essay explaining your views on assimilation.

2. The poem below describes the experiences of an immigrant who came to the United States 100 years ago. Write an essay explaining the meaning of the poem and your reaction to it. Add your own ideas and/or the experiences of your family.

A PRAYER FOR MY GRANDMOTHER

by Nora Smith

A century ago a little girl
Left a town in Latvia[1] to board
The cargo ship that took a thousand souls
Across the North Atlantic to the Golden World.

---

1. *Latvia:* a European country that borders the Baltic Sea

That's what they told her father: the streets
Were paved with gold in New York City. Or
Did it simply feel like paradise
Without the Cossack[2] devils there to beat

Their sick, steal their wheat and kill their sons?
Eva was strong at four, and when they docked
At Ellis Island[3] in July, she held
Her baby brother in her arms and won

A place for both. Years later he would die
From pneumonia, but that summer day
She opened both their shirts for the stethoscope[4]
And faced the doctor with her stubborn eyes.

And two more boys were born to share three rooms
With a toilet down the hall. There were
No toys, no furry bears to hug. She sent
The boys to play stickball in the street,
Dodging horses' hooves and vendors'[5] carts,

While she stayed upstairs to cook for all
When her mother shriveled in retreat

From the new America. I don't
Know how she learned to write in what became
The shaky hand by which she signed her name
On my birthday cards. And now I won't

Know which neighbor taught her poker, or if
She saw a game in Yankee Stadium
When Joe DiMaggio[6] played there. She died
At ninety-five last year: her fingers stiff,

Her tiny body pierced with tubes. I light
A candle by the stove and wish her peace.
I would not have been as brave as she.
She did her work. The candle burns all night.

---

2. *Cossack:* a member of a war-like people from Southern Russia who fought on horseback
   in the Russian army
3. *Ellis Island:* an island in New York harbor where new immigrants were examined and
   registered by officials from 1892–1924
4. *stethoscope:* a doctor's instrument used to listen to the chest
5. *vendor:* a person who sells food or other small items on the street out of a cart
6. *Joe DiMaggio:* a famous American baseball player, who played for the New York Yankees
   from 1936–1951

9 CASE STUDIES IN BUSINESS ETHICS: MALDEN MILLS AND BEN & JERRY'S ICE CREAM

WRITING A COMPARISON AND CONTRAST ESSAY

In this unit you will practice:
- writing a business letter
- using point-by-point organization
- writing transitional sentences

Editing focus:
- connectors showing comparison and contrast
- direct and embedded questions
- noun clauses

◆ *I* **Fluency Practice: Freewriting**

What are your ethics (your beliefs of right and wrong) and how did you form them?

In your notebook, list the factors that influenced your ethics, such as your family, friends, religion, school, books, or TV and newspapers. Write them in the order of greatest influence. Then write for ten minutes in response to the above questions. Try to express yourself as well as you can. Don't worry about mistakes. Share your writing with a partner.

The following is a short history of Malden Mills, a textile manufacturer.

MALDEN MILLS

In Massachusetts, New England, textile[1] manufacturing has been hit hard, first by domestic competition, and in the last 60 years, by
5 international competition. Many companies have moved south or overseas to reduce their labor costs and have laid off[2] thousands of workers. The most notable
10 factory still open is Malden Mills, which the Feuerstein[3] family has owned since 1906. It makes over $300 million a year, in part because the owners have invested a lot of money in R & D[4] for new products. The company invented a new
15 synthetic[5] fabric called "Polartec," a very warm, light-weight material used by retailers[6] like L.L.Bean, Land's End, and Eddie Bauer.

One night an explosion in a boiler room began a fire that injured 33 employees and caused damage estimated at $500 million. The entire Malden Mills factory burned to the ground in the largest fire
20 Massachusetts had seen in 100 years. Close to 3,200 people were put out of work just a few weeks before Christmas.

At daybreak many Malden Mills employees were distressed, some crying, convinced that their jobs were gone. Rumors spread through the city of Lawrence, Massachusetts: the mill was closing, the mill would
25 never rebuild, the mill would move somewhere else where wages were cheaper. Three days after the disaster, all the workers gathered to hear Aaron Feuerstein, the owner of the company, make a statement. "I'll get right to the announcement," he said as the workers held their breath. "For the next 30 days—it may be longer—all employees will be paid full
30 salaries. We are going to rebuild right here!" The workers stood and cheered. Both workers and the business community were astonished when Feuerstein announced again in January that he would pay them for a second month, and still once more for a third month in February.

---

1. *textile:* cloth such as wool or cotton
2. *to lay off:* to fire workers for economic reasons
3. *Feuerstein* is pronounced "FOYER-steen"
4. *R & D:* research and development
5. *synthetic:* a man-made material not found in nature
6. *retailers:* businesses that sell directly to the customer

Feuerstein's actions drew criticism from manufacturers in the garment
35 industry. The manufacturers criticized his actions as contradicting the
spirit of free enterprise.[7] Feuerstein's defenders, on the other hand,
said that he had acted in his own interest as well as his workers'.
The production of Polartec is a hands-on, difficult process that requires
specialized technology and experienced workers, so Feuerstein needs his
40 workers just as much as they need him, a fact he always admitted.
    "Some of the modern CEOs[8] ask me, 'Why did I do it?'" Feuerstein
said. "Perhaps I could have made a better deal with the insurance
companies and cashed in all the stock and all the hard labor that went
into three generations of work. But that would have been against my
45 conscience. I wish for one thing for those new CEOs who care nothing
about their workers and their communities and only think about the so-
called 'shareholder.'[9] I hope that they will wake up and change and
assume the quality of real leadership."
    Feuerstein was called a hero by the media. He disagreed with the
50 label, saying, "What has happened is that the ethics and value systems
we used to have no longer exist, so the media are giving me all kinds of
credit for this. But I haven't changed. I only did what I thought was right."
    Feuerstein has been sharing Malden Mills' prosperity with the
community for a long time. The mill has paid wages above the industry
55 average, with a full benefits package[10] for employees. In addition, the mill
and a local bank established a program to help employees buy their own
homes. Malden Mills also supports many local charities such as homeless
shelters. It also supports international charities like the Red Cross, and in
1999 Malden Mills donated 2,000 Polartec blankets to Turkey after a
60 massive earthquake. Thus, its corporate culture benefits the owners,
employees, and the community.
    During the first few days it seemed impossible that Malden Mills could
be rebuilt, but Feuerstein and his managers set to the task. Machinery
was air-freighted in, and state officials sped the process of gaining permits
65 for rebuilding. Most of all, the rebuilding was due to the great determination
of Malden Mills employees. "I can't tell you with what dedication and self-
sacrifice my management team and workforce responded," Feuerstein
later recalled. "They worked unbelievable hours to bring us back into
business." Feuerstein's concern for his workers had been repaid in kind.[11]

---

7. *free enterprise:* freedom of private business to organize and operate for profit in a
   competitive system without government interference
8. *CEO:* chief executive officer
9. *shareholder:* someone who owns stock in a business
10. *benefits package:* health insurance and old-age pensions paid in part or in total by
    employers
11. *repaid in kind:* an idiom meaning that other people will treat you as well or as badly
    as you have treated them

A. General Understanding

1. Categorizing Topics about Malden Mills

Match the topics about Malden Mills in the box next to the appropriate category below. Discuss your answers with a partner. In your notebook, write more topics from the reading so that you have three or four for each category.

a. 1906
b. workers earn enough to own homes
c. air-lift machinery
d. an explosion in the boiler room
e. family business
f. 3,200 jobs in danger
g. R&D of Polartec
h. full wages paid during rebuilding
i. gives to local charities
j. employees injured
k. full benefits package
l. workers helped rebuild business

1. Characteristics and origin of the company: <u>a, e</u>

2. Company policy toward workers: _____

3. Company policy toward the community: _____

4. Company crisis (time of great difficulty): _____

5. Company response to the crisis: _____

2. Making a Controversial Decision

In the chart below, write the effects of Mr. Feuerstein's business decisions both on his workers and the community, and on the company and its shareholders. Then imagine that it is your own company. Would you make the same decisions as Mr. Feuerstein? Discuss your answers with a partner.

Decision	Effects on Workers and Community	Effects on Company and Shareholders
1. To pay wages above the industry average to all of his workers	Workers had a good standard of living. The community shared in the prosperity.	The company had a stable work force.
2. To rebuild the factory in the same location		
3. To pay workers for three months during rebuilding		

B. Working with Language

Circle the synonym for the bolded word in each sentence. There may be more than one correct answer for a question.

1. **Executives** are people who make decisions and direct others in a company.

   a. employees
   b. senior businesspeople
   c. shareholders

2. Employees of a large corporation usually receive **benefits** along with their salaries.

   a. bonuses
   b. health insurance
   c. pension funds

3. Corporations sell **stocks** to investors in order to raise money for expansion. The investors receive payments when the company makes a profit.

   a. shares of a company
   b. dividends
   c. checks

4. In contrast to that of Malden Mills, the **corporate culture** of some companies emphasizes making money for shareholders without regard to the interests of workers or the larger community.

   a. policy of the company
   b. financial status of the company
   c. publicity for the company

5. Some companies cut their **staff** to make extra money for shareholders, even sometimes when the economy is good.

   a. work force
   b. dividends
   c. expenses

6. When companies **downsize**, they sometimes lay off even loyal executives who have worked for the company for a long time.

   a. promote employees
   b. hire employees
   c. reduce the size of the company

III ▶ Prewriting Activities

The following reading is an account of the history of Ben & Jerry's Homemade, Inc., a manufacturer of ice cream.

BEN & JERRY'S GETS SCOOPED UP

Ben & Jerry's Homemade, Inc., was founded in 1978 by Ben Cohen and Jerry Greenfield, two childhood
5 friends who each paid five dollars for a correspondence course[1] in ice-cream making and opened their first ice-cream store in a renovated
10 gas station in Vermont,

Ben & Jerry's original store

New England. Ben and Jerry promised to make a high-quality product: ice cream made from milk from local family farms with no chemical hormones.[2] Their idea was to produce chunky, rich ice cream with natural ingredients and unusual new flavors. The idea worked! To finance the
15 growth of their company, Ben and Jerry sold company shares for small amounts of money to local people in Vermont.

To show their esteem[3] for all of their employees, Ben and Jerry followed the advice of *The Republic,* written by the ancient Greek philosopher Plato: the difference between the highest and the lowest paid workers
20 would be in a ratio of 5:1.[4] Unlike companies that gave its CEOs up to 300 times the salary of the lowest-paid workers, Ben & Jerry's gave the highest paid executive only five times the salary of the lowest paid employee. In this way, the co-founders felt that everyone's contribution to the company would be respected. To involve all of its employees in
25 expanding and improving the company, Ben and Jerry created a corporate culture of relative equality, where every worker could make suggestions, express an opinion, and earn a livable wage.

In addition to respecting its employees, Ben & Jerry's believes that business must play an important role in helping the local, national, and
30 international community. Ben & Jerry's gives away 7.5 percent of its pre-tax earnings to support charitable projects that help the poor and

---

1. *correspondence course:* course of study done at home using mail or the Internet
2. *chemical hormone:* man-made substance given to cows to increase milk production
3. *esteem:* respect
4. *5:1:* five to one

protect the planet. For example, Ben & Jerry's has made contracts with suppliers who offered jobs to the homeless in the United States. Ben & Jerry's has also supported programs for literacy, community clean-ups,
35 and world peace. The co-founders call this attention to natural products, employee welfare, and charity work "caring capitalism."

Ben & Jerry's was remarkably successful for almost 20 years, but by the
40 end of the 20th century, the company faced many problems. First, it had become increasingly difficult to recruit executives
45 with the 5:1 salary ratio because executives could get much higher salaries elsewhere. The second problem Ben & Jerry's had
50 was that it changed its method of distribution[5], so it had difficulty delivering its ice cream to the customer. Last but not least, the price
55 of the company's stock had

Ben Cohen and Jerry Greenfield

not performed as well as its shareholders had hoped. For all these reasons, the company was obliged to sell. It made an agreement with Unilever, a large multinational corporation, to buy Ben & Jerry's. Unilever expanded Ben & Jerry's ice cream as a global brand in many countries,
60 but Unilever said it would maintain Ben & Jerry's as an independent entity, allowing the ice-cream maker to continue its social activism.

Unilever also promised that it would continue to make Ben & Jerry's ice cream only in Vermont. And Ben & Jerry's employees still receive the fringe benefit of three free pints of ice cream per week. More important,
65 Unilever agreed to continue giving 7.5 percent of all pre-tax profits from Ben & Jerry's to charity.

The owners of Ben & Jerry's hope that a little David can transform a multinational Goliath,[6] and that "caring capitalism" can continue to do good work.

---

5. *distribution:* the transport of supplies and products to various people or places
6. *David and Goliath:* David was a young shepherd in the Bible who saved his people from the giant Goliath and defeated him.

A. General Understanding

1. Categorizing Topics about Ben & Jerry's

Match the topics about Ben & Jerry's in the box next to the appropriate category below. Discuss your answers with a partner. In your notebook, write more topics from the reading so that you have three or four for each category.

a. 5:1 wages	g. sold shares to local people to finance the business
b. correspondence course	h. workers can make suggestions
c. 7.5 percent profits to charity	i. sold to Unilever
d. problem recruiting executives	j. had difficulty with distribution
e. employees earn a livable wage	k. will expand its markets and become a global brand
f. supports Vermont dairy farmers by buying milk from local family farms	l. company's stock had not performed well

1. Characteristics and origin of the company: _b, f_

2. Company policy toward workers: _____

3. Company policy toward the community: _____

4. Crisis in the company: _____

5. Company response to the crisis: _____

B. Business Ethics

Complete this chart with your responses to the question below. Then share your answers with a partner.

Suppose you were offered an executive position with a salary of $300,000 a year from one of the companies described below. Would you refuse or accept this offer?

Company Description	Refuse offer	Accept offer	Not Sure
A company that has dumped toxic pollutants in the local river in the past			
A tobacco company			
A factory where workers have been seriously injured			

Consider whether unethical activity occurs in these institutions and occupations. Rank each starting with 1 for the greatest occurrence of unethical activity. Discuss your answers with a small group. Explain your reasoning. Give examples that you know or have read about.

_____ Banking _____ Manufacturing _____ Law

_____ Construction _____ Government _____ Sales

_____ Media _____ Medicine _____ Accounting

C. Point-of-View Writing

Write a business letter to Ben & Jerry's. Use the address 30 Community Drive, South Burlington, Vermont 05403. Explain that you would like to open a Ben & Jerry's in your neighborhood. First read the letter below and use it as a model to help you.

Your address →
Cooper Dry Goods Store
14 Mill Pond Lane
Colorado Springs, Colorado 80901

Date →
August 4, 2003

Company address →
Orders Department
Malden Mills
520 Broadway
Lawrence, Massachusetts 01841

Salutation →
Dear Customer Service:

Body of the letter →
We would like to order 20 Polartec vests, item number 45678, half in men's medium and half in men's large sizes. Delivery must be made no later than September 1 so that we can take advantage of the fall buying season. Enclosed is our deposit. We are happy to be placing our first order with your company. Our family, which runs our store, read about your efforts to stand by your workers and rebuild the factory after that devastating fire. My wife and I admire the way you run your business, and we would be proud to carry your products. We know that our customers will appreciate a warm, well-made garment for our cold Colorado winters. We look forward to more business with you in the future.

Closing →
Sincerely,

Signature →
Tom Drayton

Printed name →
Tom Drayton

Ⅳ Structured Writing Focus

Compare and contrast Malden Mills and Ben & Jerry's in a five-paragraph essay. Use these three points: the companies' policies toward employees, their policies toward their local communities, and their contributions to charities.

ALTERNATIVE TASK: Write a five-paragraph essay comparing and contrasting two other companies, for example, Starbucks and Dunkin' Donuts, or two types of businesses, for example, the entertainment industry and the media. Write about three points, such as company ethics or business organization.

A. Starting to Write

1. Before You Brainstorm: Using Point-by-Point Organization

When you write a comparison and contrast essay on two complex subjects, it is best to use a **point-by-point organization**: in each paragraph you compare your subjects on one **point.** Discuss the subjects in the same order for each paragraph.

2. Brainstorming

Working with a partner, write notes on two points of comparison between Malden Mills and Ben & Jerry's or two other companies. For each point of comparison, write similarities and differences between the companies. Write in your notebook using the model to help you.

Point of Comparison	Similarities	Differences
The companies' response to a crises	Both companies solved a financial crisis with ethical decisions.	MM decided to rebuild the factory and pay salaries to idle workers, despite criticism from the industry. Ben & Jerry's decided to sell the company to Unilever on the condition that Unilever continue giving 7.5 percent of pretax profits to charity.

B. Preparing the First Draft

1. Thesis Statements for Comparison and Contrast Essays

In a comparison and contrast essay, the thesis statement must show your position on the topic—it can not merely compare two subjects.

Put a check (✔) next to the sentences below that could be effective thesis statements in a comparison and contrast essay.

_____ 1. "There are advantages and disadvantages to both large supermarkets and small grocery stores."

_____ 2. "Although small grocery stores are very convenient, they are quite expensive."

_____ 3. "Although small grocery stores are more convenient than supermarkets because groceries are often open all day and night, they can never match the variety or the high sales volume of large supermarket chains."

Put a check (✔) next to the main idea of these thesis statements about businesses.

1. "Although prices are higher in small grocery stores than they are in large supermarkets, some people prefer shopping in small groceries because they give personal service and offer a greater selection of international foods."

    Main idea: _____ Small groceries are better.

    _____ Large supermarkets are better.

2. "Despite the fact that department stores are less convenient than catalogues, department stores give people greater choice and allow them to try on clothes before buying them."

    Main idea: _____ Mail-order catalogues are better.

    _____ Department stores are better.

3. "Owning an independent restaurant allows a person more creativity and individuality. However, owning a restaurant franchise, such as KFC or Taco Bell, involves less financial risk and includes management training."

    Main idea: _____ Franchise restaurants are better.

    _____ Independent restaurants are better.

2. Organizing Ideas from the Thesis Statement

Discuss with a partner how you would organize the ideas from thesis statements 2 and 3 in the previous exercise. Draw boxes in your notebook and write the topics for each body paragraph that would follow in an essay. Thesis statement 1 has been done for you.

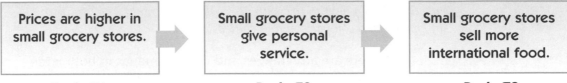

Prices are higher in small grocery stores.	Small grocery stores give personal service.	Small grocery stores sell more international food.
Body ¶1	**Body ¶2**	**Body ¶3**

3. Transitional Sentences

Transitional sentences connect ideas logically. They remind the reader of ideas from the last paragraph and they introduce ideas that come in the next paragraph. A transitional sentence can be the first or last sentence of a body paragraph or it may be an internal transition within a paragraph.

Read this excerpt from an essay on small grocery stores and study the transitional sentences in bold. Then complete the exercise on the next page.

Transitional sentence → **Despite the financial drawback, some people still prefer small neighborhood grocery stores because they provide personal service.** Unlike supermarkets, grocery stores have few employees and are often owned and run by one family. While supermarket shoppers are usually treated as just another faceless customer, grocery store shoppers are often recognized, or even greeted by name, when they enter the store. As a result, shoppers look forward to this friendly *Internal transition* → family atmosphere. **The personal service of grocery stores is also reflected in their general convenience.** Not only are small groceries located close to people's homes, but in many cases they are open 24 *Concluding sentence* → hours a day or until midnight. **But this is not the only advantage grocery stores have.**

Transitional sentence → In addition to their personal service and convenience, grocery stores offer a choice of foods that can satisfy the tastes and needs of the different groups of people that live in the community . . .

PRACTICE SELECTING TRANSITIONAL SENTENCES

Match the transitional sentences with their locations in the two body paragraphs. Write each transitional sentence on the lines provided. When you have finished, compare your answers with a partner's and discuss which transitional sentences argue for or against shopping at department stores.

TRANSITIONAL SENTENCES

a. **Even though department stores require customers to go to the store, department stores have a great advantage over catalogues: customers know that the clothing they buy fits them.**

b. **Despite the flexible hours of department stores, some people simply lack the time to go shopping.**

c. **In addition to being able to see themselves in a mirror, department store customers also enjoy being able to touch and feel the merchandise.**

BODY PARAGRAPHS

1. _____

_____

_____

Some people are so busy during working hours that they cannot go shopping when department stores are open. With mail-order catalogues, they can do all of their shopping at home and place their orders at any time during the day or night.

2. _____

_____

_____

People have no idea if the clothes they select from catalogues will fit well. In contrast, when they buy clothes at a department store, they can try the clothing on first and be confident that their purchase will fit.

3. _____

_____

_____

Customers can run their fingers through articles of clothing or touch textiles and furniture. This pleasant sensory experience is yet another advantage of shopping in a department store.

4. Organizing Your Essay

Study this block diagram of a five-paragraph essay to plan a first draft of your essay. In your notebook, draw your own diagram and write your notes in each of its sections.

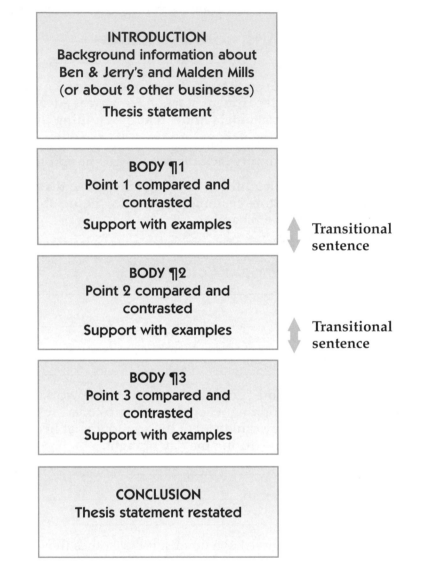

INTRODUCTION
Background information about
Ben & Jerry's and Malden Mills
(or about 2 other businesses)
Thesis statement

BODY ¶1
Point 1 compared and
contrasted
Support with examples

Transitional
sentence

BODY ¶2
Point 2 compared and
contrasted
Support with examples

Transitional
sentence

BODY ¶3
Point 3 compared and
contrasted
Support with examples

CONCLUSION
Thesis statement restated

*Now write a **first draft** of your essay. Remember to write in complete sentences, and try to use some of the vocabulary and structures that you have practiced in this unit.*

C. Revising the First Draft

When you have finished writing the first draft, read it to a partner.

CHECKLIST FOR REVISING THE FIRST DRAFT

When you listen to your partner's essay and discuss your own, keep these questions in mind:

1. Does the introduction give background information about the two businesses being compared?

2. Does the thesis statement identify the three points to be compared and contrasted in the three body paragraphs?

3. Does each body paragraph discuss a different point of comparison and contrast?

4. Is the essay logically organized? Are there transitional sentences between the ideas? from one paragraph to another? within the body paragraphs?

5. Are there appropriate examples for each point of comparison and contrast?

6. Is the thesis restated in the conclusion?

After discussing your essay with a partner, some reorganization may be necessary.

*Now write a **second draft** that includes all of your additions and changes.*

D. Editing the Second Draft

After you have written a second draft, proofread your work for any errors and correct them. These guidelines and exercises should help.

1. Connectors Showing Comparison and Contrast*

COMPARISON

both	like	similarly	just as
and	similar to	in the same way	in the same way that
	the same as		

CONTRAST

but	unlike	in contrast	whereas
yet	different from	however	while
		nevertheless	although /even though
			despite / despite the fact that

EXAMPLES OF COMPARISON / CONTRAST SENTENCES

The marketing strategies of mail-order catalogues are **similar to** the marketing strategies of department stores.

Mail-order catalogues are **different from** department stores in several aspects. For one, they are more convenient to shoppers.

Department stores depend on strong sales during the holiday season. **Similarly,** mail order catalogues count on heavy holiday sales.

Department stores offer discounts to customers who use their store credit card. **In the same way,** some mail-order catalogues lower costs for people who use their company credit card.

Unlike department stores, which give their customers personal service, mail-order catalogues are impersonal.

Department stores sometimes do not offer much privacy; **in contrast,** mail-order catalogues give customers complete privacy. **Nevertheless**, department stores are very popular.

---

*See the following pages to review these expressions: *but, however, while,* and *like* (Unit 3, page 43); *the same as, compared with / as opposed to,* and *different from* (Unit 3, page 51); *despite / despite the fact that* (Unit 8, page 154), and *although / even though* (Unit 8, page 155).

Rewrite each of these sentences comparing Ben & Jerry's ice cream to Malden Mills' Polartec. Write sentences using the connectors in parentheses. It may be necessary to change the wording of some sentences. Reorganize, but do not change the meaning. When you have finished, compare your answers with a partner's.

1. Polartec is a man-made fiber, whereas Ben & Jerry's ice cream is made from all-natural ingredients. *(in contrast, unlike)*

   Polartec is a man-made fiber; in contrast, Ben & Jerry's

   ice cream is made from all-natural ingredients.

   Unlike Polartec, which is a man-made fiber, Ben & Jerry's

   ice cream is made from all-natural ingredients.

2. Malden Mills sends Polartec to factories before it comes to stores. **In contrast**, Ben & Jerry's sends its ice cream directly to food stores. *(while, unlike)*

   _____

   _____

   _____

3. **Despite the fact that** Polartec and Ben & Jerry's ice cream are different kinds of products, the companies that make them have a lot in common. *(although, nevertheless)*

   _____

   _____

   _____

4. **Both** Polartec and Ben & Jerry's ice cream appeal to the senses. *(like, similarly)*

   _____

   _____

   _____

2. Direct Questions and Embedded Questions

DIRECT QUESTIONS

Direct questions use **inverted subject-verb word order** when you know the subject but you are asking about its circumstance, time, place, or manner. In this type of direct question, the auxiliary comes before the subject. If there is no auxiliary, the main verb *be* comes before the subject.

What	do	the companies	sell?
When	did	the companies	succeed?
Why	have	the companies	succeeded?
QUESTION WORD	(AUXILIARY)	SUBJECT	MAIN VERB
How	are	the companies	different?
QUESTION WORD	BE	SUBJECT	

EMBEDDED QUESTIONS

Embedded questions are also called indirect questions. They always use regular subject-verb word order.

I want to know	**what**	the companies	sell.
Is it clear	**when**	the companies	succeeded?
Do you know	**why**	the companies	have succeeded?
Could you explain	**how**	the companies	are different?
	QUESTION WORD	SUBJECT	(AUXILIARY) MAIN VERB

Working with a partner, change these questions from direct to embedded questions. Start your sentences with expressions like the ones in the box above.

1. Why is it important for both employers and employees to get along?

   I would like to know why it is important for both employers
   and employees to get along.

2. When should an employer consider the needs of the community?

   _____

   _____

3. Where should an employer of a local factory do his recruiting?

_____

_____

4. What should employees expect from their employers?

_____

_____

5. What is the best proof of an employee's loyalty?

_____

_____

6. How can employers get the best work from their employees?

_____

_____

3. Noun Clauses

Noun clauses replace nouns and can be used as subjects, complements, and objects. They are often introduced by *what* or *how*. They have the same structure as embedded questions.

<u>What Ben & Jerry's has in common with Malden Mills</u> is its "caring capitalism."
    SUBJECT

Caring capitalism is <u>what Ben & Jerry's has in common with Malden Mills.</u>
                    COMPLEMENT

Many companies want to know <u>how they can win their employees' respect.</u>
                    OBJECT

<u>How Ben & Jerry's and Malden Mills won their employee's respect</u> was to
        SUBJECT
treat them fairly.

The noun clauses below are the subjects of each sentence. Complete each sentence with your opinion. Use noun clauses when possible. When you have finished, share your sentences with a partner.

1. How much money a company contributes to the community is . . .

   <u>How much money a company contributes to the community</u>
   <u>expresses what its values are.</u>

2. How much respect a company gives to its employees determines . . .

   _____

   _____

3. Whoever supervises people at the workplace should be . . .

   _____

   _____

4. What corporations should do for better public relations is . . .

   _____

   _____

5. How Malden Mills employees responded to the crisis was . . .

   _____

   _____

Read these paragraphs on a fictitious person. Working with a partner, put a check (✓) above the bolded words that are correct. Cross out the words that are incorrect and write your corrections above them. There are five more errors.

✓
What the owners of Ben & Jerry's and Malden Mills have in common

is their concern for their employees' welfare. Employers who know

why it is important
~~why is it important~~ to respect their employees understand **what is "caring**

capitalism" all about. David Bennett had just this kind of understanding

when he opened his seafood restaurant, the Neptune King, in Baltimore,

Maryland.

Mr. Bennett had taught courses in business at several restaurant schools. **What had he always told** his students is that people are honest, and loyal, and that employers should regard their employees as trustworthy. So when he opened his restaurant, **what he was eager to put into practice** was **what had he preached.** However, in the first few years of running his restaurant, he learned that **what did he believe in** was not necessarily true.

Mr. Bennett had hired a group of **what he considered to be honest, trustworthy, and loyal employees,** but not all of them were honest. **What some of them did** was cheat him in many ways, by taking his most expensive seafood and stealing money.

Despite these difficulties, Mr. Bennett refused to abandon his philosophy that people are essentially good. First, he started over his business with new employees. Then **what he set out to do** was to change the general state of employee-employer relations in the restaurant industry and thus win his employees' loyalty. **How has he done this** has been by showing his employees that he cares about their futures by offering them stock options and career opportunities.

E. Preparing the Final Draft

Reread your second draft and correct any errors you find. Put a check (✓) in each space as you edit for these points. Then write your corrected final version.

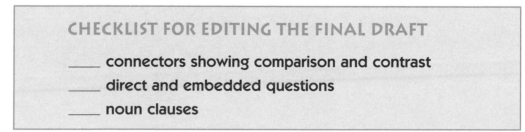

CHECKLIST FOR EDITING THE FINAL DRAFT

_____ **connectors showing comparison and contrast**
_____ **direct and embedded questions**
_____ **noun clauses**

Additional Writing Opportunities

Write about one of the following topics.

1. Watch one of these films about business and write an essay telling how the business problem in the film was solved. How realistic was the film's treatment of business issues?

   You've Got Mail: the struggle of a small independent bookstore against a large chain store

   Wall Street: ethical issues in the world of finance

   It's a Wonderful Life: the story of a small-town building and loan company and its struggle against a big bank

   Gung Ho: a comedy about an American company taken over by a Japanese firm

2. Write a five-paragraph essay in which you compare and contrast the values you learned from two influences: your family, school, religion, friends, books, or the media. How are the values different? Do you agree with the values of one group more than those of the others? Do you disagree with any of the values that you encountered?

3. Research another company that practices "caring capitalism" like Malden Mills and Ben & Jerry's. Some well-known companies are Paul Newman, Inc., and The Body Shop. Then write a five-paragraph essay on the company. Consider the following issues: Why is it socially responsible? Does it care most about the local community, the environment, its workers, or another issue? What difficulties has the company faced? Do you agree with the company's philosophy and its business practices?

4. You want to start your own business. Decide what business you would want, for example, a neighborhood store, a restaurant, an Internet company, a day-care center, a mechanic's garage, a tutoring service. Choose the location and describe the start-up money you would need and where you would get that money. How would you run the business? Write a five-paragraph essay about your plans to start the business of your dreams.

WRITING AN ESSAY ANALYZING LITERATURE

In this unit you will practice:

- writing about plot, climax, narrative point of view, characters, setting, pace, mood, foreshadowing, irony, and theme
- supporting your interpretation with references and citations

Editing focus:

- cause and effect with *such . . . that / so . . . that*
- simple present and simple past verbs in an essay on literature

 I Fluency Practice: Predicting and Freewriting

> "True!—nervous—very, very dreadfully nervous I had been and am; but why *will* you say that I am mad? The disease had sharpened my senses— not destroyed—not dulled them. Above all was the sense of hearing acute. I heard all things in the heaven and in the earth. I heard many things in hell. How, then, am I mad? Hearken! and observe how healthily—how calmly I can tell you the whole story."

This is the first paragraph of Edgar Allan Poe's short story, "The Tell-Tale Heart." What is the narrator (the storyteller and, in this story, the main character) saying to the reader in this first paragraph? What do you think the story is going to be about?

Write for ten minutes in answer to these questions. Then read what you wrote to a partner.

II ▸ Reading for Writing

Edgar Allan Poe (1809–1849) is one of the
world's greatest short story writers. He is
considered the inventor of the detective story,
for example, "The Purloined Letter" and "The
Murders in the Rue Morgue." He also wrote
tales of suspense and terror such as this story,
"The Tell Tale Heart."[1] Poe had a tragic life.
His parents died when he was two years old.
He was raised, but never officially adopted, by
a wealthy merchant named John Allan, who
never understood him. Poe's beloved wife,
Virginia Clemm, died very young. Poe himself
died at 40, a victim of poverty, alcoholism, and
some say a brain tumor.

THE TELL-TALE HEART
by Edgar Allan Poe

True!—nervous—very, very dreadfully nervous I had
been and am; but why will you say that I am <u>mad</u>? The
disease had sharpened my senses—not destroyed—not
dulled them. Above all was the sense of hearing <u>acute</u>.
5 I heard all things in the heaven and in the earth. I heard
many things in hell. How, then, am I mad? <u>Hearken</u>! and
observe how healthily—how calmly I can tell you the
whole story.

It is impossible to say how first the idea entered my
10 brain; but, once conceived, it haunted me day and night.
<u>Object</u> there was none. Passion there was none. I loved the
old man. He had never wronged me. He had never given
me insult. For his gold I had no desire. I think it was his
eye! Yes, it was this! One of his eyes resembled that of a
15 <u>vulture</u>—a pale blue eye, with a <u>film</u> over it. Whenever it fell
upon me, my blood ran cold; and so by degrees—very
gradually—I made up my mind to take the life of the old
man, and thus rid myself of the eye forever.

Now this is the point. You think me mad. Madmen know
20 nothing. But you should have seen *me*. You should have
seen how wisely I <u>proceeded</u>—with what caution—with
what planning—with what <u>dissimulation</u> I went to work!
I was never kinder to the old man than during the whole

mad: crazy

acute: sharp

hearken: listen

object: purpose

vulture: a bird that eats dead animals

film: a cataract; clouding of the eye, which damages vision

proceeded: continued

dissimulation: hiding one's feelings

---

1. This reading has been slightly abridged and some of the difficult
vocabulary has been altered.

week before I killed him. And every night, about midnight,
25 I turned the lock of his door and opened it—oh, so gently!
And then, when I had made an opening sufficient for my
head, I put in a dark lantern, all closed, closed, so that no
light shone out, and then I thrust in my head. Oh, you
would have laughed to see how cunningly I pushed my
30 head in! I moved it slowly—very, very slowly so that I might
not disturb the old man's sleep. It took me an hour to place
my whole head within the opening so far that I could see
him as he lay upon his bed. Ha!—would a madman have
been so wise as this? And then, when my head was well in
35 the room, I undid the lantern cautiously (for the hinges
creaked)—I undid it just so much that a single thin ray fell
upon the vulture eye. And this I did for seven long nights—
every night just at midnight—but I found the eye always
closed; and so it was impossible to do the work; for it was
40 not the old man who angered me, but this Evil Eye.[2] And
every morning, when the day broke, I went boldly into the
chamber, and spoke courageously to him, calling him by
name in a hearty tone, and inquiring how he had passed
the night. So you see he would have been a very profound
45 old man, indeed, to suspect that every night, just at 12, I
looked in upon him while he slept.

   Upon the eighth night I was more than usually cautious
in opening the door. A watch's minute hand moves more
quickly than did mine. Never, before that night, had I *felt*
50 the extent of my own powers—of my sagacity. I could
scarcely contain my feelings of triumph.[3] To think that there
I was, opening the door, little by little, and he not even to
dream of my secret deeds or thoughts. I fairly chuckled at
the idea; and perhaps he heard me; for he moved on the
55 bed suddenly, as if startled. Now you may think that I drew
back—but no. His room was as black as pitch with the thick
darkness (for the windows were close fastened, through fear
of robbers), and so I knew that he could not see the opening
of the door, and I kept pushing it on steadily, steadily.

continued

lantern: a hand-held gas lamp

thrust: pushed

cunningly: cleverly

hinges: joints on the windows of the lantern

creaked: made a scraping sound

hearty: friendly

sagacity: wisdom

chuckled: laughed

drew back: moved back

---

2. *evil eye:* superstition from 3,000 B.C. that some people can hurt or destroy
   others with a glance
3. *I could scarcely contain my feelings of triumph:* My feelings were so strong
   they almost escaped my control.

60   I had my head in, and was about to open the lantern,
when my finger slipped upon the tin fastening, and the
old man sprang up in the bed, crying out—"Who's there?"

    I kept quite still and said nothing. For a whole hour I
did not move a muscle, and in the meantime I did not hear
65 him lie down. He was still sitting up in the bed listening;—
just as I have done, night after night, harkening to the
death-watches[4] in the wall.

    Presently I heard a slight <u>groan</u>, and I knew it was the   *groan:* cry of pain
groan of deadly terror. It was not a groan of pain or of
70 <u>grief</u>—oh, no!—it was the low <u>stifled</u> sound that arises from   *grief:* sadness
the bottom of the soul when overcharged with fear. I knew   *stifled:* held back
the sound well. I knew what the old man felt, and <u>pitied</u>   *pitied:* felt sorry for
him, although I chuckled at heart. I knew that he had been
lying awake ever since the first slight noise, when he had
75 turned in the bed. His fears had been ever since growing
upon him. He had been trying to imagine them causeless,
but could not. He had been trying to say to himself—"it is
nothing but the wind in the chimney—it is only a mouse
crossing the floor." Yes, he had been trying to comfort
80 himself with these ideas: but he found all useless.
All useless, because Death in approaching him, had
<u>stalked</u> him with his black shadow before him, and   *stalked:* hunted
enveloped the victim.

To Be Continued . . .

---

4. The *deathwatch* beetle is a small insect that makes holes in old wood.
   According to superstition, the clicking sound it makes is a warning
   of death.

A. General Understanding

1. Setting the Stage

*Write answers to these questions based on the reading. Write your answers in your
notebook and then discuss what you have written with a partner.*

1. What does the narrator want to do? Why?

2. How does the narrator spy on the old man?

3. Why can't the narrator carry out his plan?

4. How does the narrator hide his feelings every morning?

5. Why does the old man wake up when the narrator enters his room?

6. Why is the old man terrified?

Continue reading "The Tell-Tale Heart," and then complete the tasks that follow.

When I had waited a long time, very patiently, without
hearing him lie down, I decided to open a little—a very,
very little <u>crevice</u> in the lantern. So I opened it—you cannot
imagine how stealthily, <u>stealthily</u>,—until, at last, a single
dim ray of light, like the thread of the spider, shot from out
the crevice and fell upon the vulture eye.

crevice: small opening

stealthily: secretly

It was open—wide, wide open—and I grew furious as I
<u>gazed</u> upon it. I saw it with perfect clearness—all a dull
blue, with a horrible veil over it that <u>chilled</u> the very marrow
in my bones; but I could see nothing
else of the old man's face or person
because I had directed the ray as if
by instinct, precisely on the damned
spot.

gazed: looked at

chilled: made very cold

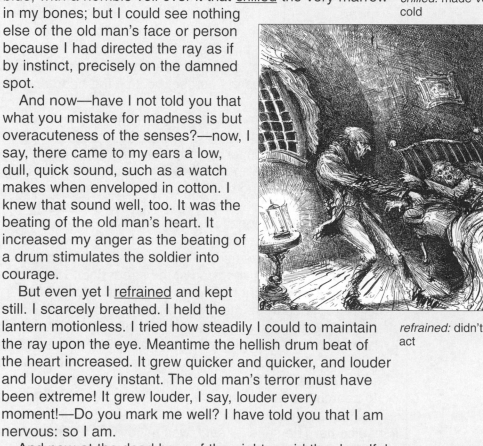

And now—have I not told you that
what you mistake for madness is but
overacuteness of the senses?—now, I
say, there came to my ears a low,
dull, quick sound, such as a watch
makes when enveloped in cotton. I
knew that sound well, too. It was the
beating of the old man's heart. It
increased my anger as the beating of
a drum stimulates the soldier into
courage.

But even yet I <u>refrained</u> and kept
still. I scarcely breathed. I held the
lantern motionless. I tried how steadily I could to maintain
the ray upon the eye. Meantime the hellish drum beat of
the heart increased. It grew quicker and quicker, and louder
and louder every instant. The old man's terror must have
been extreme! It grew louder, I say, louder every
moment!—Do you mark me well? I have told you that I am
nervous: so I am.

refrained: didn't act

And now at the <u>dead hour of the night</u>, amid the dreadful
silence of that old house, so strange a noise as this excited
me to uncontrollable terror. Yet, for some minutes longer I
refrained and stood still.

dead hour of the night: midnight

But the beating grew louder, louder! I thought the heart
might burst. And now I became anxious again—the sound
would be heard by a neighbor! The old man's hour had come!

continued

The Tell-Tale Heart   185

125 With a loud yell, I threw open the lantern and leaped into
the room. He shrieked once—once only. In an instant I
dragged him to the floor, and pulled the heavy bed over
him. I then smiled gaily, to find the deed so far done. But,
for many minutes, the heart beat on with a muffled sound.
130 This, however, did not vex me; it would not be heard
through the wall. At length it ceased. The old man was
dead. I removed the bed and then examined the corpse.
Yes, he was stone, stone dead. I placed my hand upon his
heart and held it there many minutes. There was no
135 pulsation. He was stone dead. His eye would trouble me no
more.

   If still you think me mad, you will think so no longer when
I describe the wise precautions I took to hide the body.
The night waned, and I worked hastily, but in silence. First
140 of all I dismembered the corpse. I cut off the head and the
arms and the legs.

   I then took up three planks from the flooring of the
chamber, and deposited all between the scantlings. I then
replaced the boards so cleverly, so cunningly, that no
145 human eye—not even his—could have detected anything
wrong. There was nothing to wash out—no stain of any
kind—no blood spot whatever. I had been too wary for
that. A tub had caught it all—ha! ha!

   When I had made an end to these labors, it was four
150 o'clock—still dark as midnight. As the bell sounded the
hour, there came a knocking at the street door. I went down
to open it with a light heart,—for what had I *now* to fear?
There entered three men, who introduced themselves with
perfect politeness, as officers of the police. A shriek had
155 been heard by a neighbor during the night; suspicion of foul
play had been aroused; information had been lodged at the
police office, and they (the officers) had been sent
to search the house.

   I smiled—for what had I to fear? I made the gentlemen
160 welcome. The shriek, I said, was my own in a dream. The
old man, I mentioned, was absent in the country. I took my
visitors all over the house. I told them to search—search
well. I led them, at length, to *his* chamber. I showed them
his treasures, secure, undisturbed. In the enthusiasm of my
165 confidence, I brought chairs into the room, and desired
them *here* to rest from their fatigues, while I myself placed
my own seat upon the very spot beneath which lay the
corpse of the victim.

To Be Continued . . .

shrieked: screamed

muffled: quieted
vex: make angry
ceased: stopped

the night waned:
night became
morning

*deposited all
between the
scantlings:* placed
under the floor

wary: careful

foul play: a crime

*desired them here
to rest from their
fatigues:* asked
them to sit down to
rest

2. Summarizing Events

In your notebook, write a short paragraph summarizing what has happened so far in the story. Share your summary with a partner.

3. Analyzing the Main Ideas of the Story

Read these questions. Write the line numbers of the story in which the answers can be found. Then answer the questions in your own words. Discuss your answers with a partner.

1. What is the narrator's motive for the killing of the old man?

   Line numbers: 9–19

   The motive isn't anger, money, or revenge. The narrator says he likes the old man. They had a good relationship. He kills his victim because he thinks that the old man has an evil eye. In fact, the old man's eye only has a milky cataract from old age.

2. Why does the narrator wait a week to commit his crime?

   Line numbers: _____

   _____

   _____

   _____

3. What finally drives the narrator to kill the old man?

   Line numbers: _____

   _____

   _____

   _____

4. How does the narrator kill the old man?

   Line numbers: _____

   _____

   _____

   _____

5. How does he get rid of the body?

   Line numbers: _____

   _____

   _____

   _____

6. When does the narrator first show that he may be mad?

   Line numbers: _____

   _____

   _____

   _____

7. The narrator thinks that the reader will believe that he is mad. How does the narrator argue that he is not mad? Is his argument convincing?

   Line numbers: _____

   _____

   _____

   _____

8. Why do the policemen come to the house?

   Line numbers: _____

   _____

   _____

   _____

4. Finishing the Story

Write an ending to the story in your notebook by looking back at the story and guessing the ending from the events. Then read your ending to a partner.

B. Working with Language

Working with a partner, underline the two synonyms for each word in bold. Use a dictionary if necessary.

1. **acute**	dull	sharp	very sensitive
2. **cunning**	clever	crafty	foolish
3. **dissimulation**	fakery	falsehood	truth
4. **dreadful**	attractive	shocking	terrible
5. **gazed**	disregarded	looked	stared
6. **stealthily**	openly	quietly	secretly
7. **wary**	careful	careless	watchful

Complete these sentences with one of the words in bold from the previous exercise. After you have finished, share your answers with a partner.

1. When the old man __gazed__ at the narrator, his eye frightened the narrator, who then felt he had to destroy it.

2. The narrator thought that he was very _____ in his planning of the murder.

3. The narrator's kindness to the old man was not real—it was

   _____ .

4. The narrator _____ entered the room to take his victim by surprise.

5. The narrator was very _____ of getting caught when he first put his head in the door of the old man's room.

6. When the narrator said that he had very _____ senses, he meant that he could hear the old man's heart beating.

7. The old man moaned in terror before he was killed in a _____ way.

III ▸ Prewriting Activities

Read the end of "The Tell-Tale Heart" and complete the task that follows.

The officers were satisfied.
170 My behavior had convinced them. I was strangely at ease. They sat, and while I answered cheerily, they <u>chatted</u> of familiar things. But before long, I felt
175 myself <u>getting pale</u> and wished them gone. My heart ached, and I <u>fancied</u> a ringing in my ears: but still they sat and still chatted. The ringing became
180 more clear—it continued and became much clearer: I talked more freely to get rid of the feeling, but it continued and gained definiteness—until, at length, I found that the noise was not within my ears.

185   No doubt I now grew *very* pale, but I talked more fluently, and with <u>a heightened voice</u>. Yet the sound increased—and what could I do? It was *a low, dull, quick sound—much like a sound as a watch makes when enveloped in cotton*. I gasped for breath—and yet the
190 officers heard it not. I talked more quickly—more forcefully; but the noise steadily increased. I arose and argued about unimportant things, in a high key and with violent gestures; but the noise steadily increased. Why *would* they not be gone? I paced the floor to and fro with heavy <u>strides</u>, as if
195 excited to fury by the observations of the men—but the noise steadily increased. Oh God! What *could* I do? I foamed—I shouted—I swore! I swung the chair upon which I had been sitting, and grated it upon the boards, but the noise arose over all and continually increased. It grew
200 louder—louder—*louder!* And still the men chatted pleasantly and smiled. Was it possible they heard not? Almighty God!—no! no! They heard!—they suspected!— they *knew!*—they were making a mockery of my horror!— this I thought, and this I think. But anything was better than
205 this suffering and agony! Anything was more tolerable than this <u>derision</u>! I could bear those hypocritical smiles no

chatted: talked

to become pale: to lose color in one's face from shock or sickness

fancied: imagined

a heightened voice: a louder and more forceful voice

strides: large steps

derision (deride: to make fun of someone)

longer! I felt that I must scream or die—and now—again!—
hark! louder! louder! louder! *louder!*—"Villains!" I shrieked,
"<u>dissemble</u> no more! I admit the <u>deed</u>!—tear up the planks!
210 hear! hear!—it is the beating of his <u>hideous</u> heart."

dissemble: pretend

deed: action

hideous: filling the mind with horror

The End

A. Comparing Versions of a Story

Compare the end of Poe's story with the ending you imagined. What events and ideas did you show in your version? What events and ideas does Poe's version contain? Write about the similarities or differences below. If you need more room, write in your notebook. When you have finished, share your writing with a partner.

_____

_____

_____

_____

B. Understanding Plot

The **plot** is the series of events in a story. These events traditionally take place according to this pattern:

1. **Introduction of the conflict:** the presentation of the conflict. The conflict can be characters struggling with themselves, others, or an outside force like nature.

2. **Rising action:** the events that occur before the climax. During the rising action, the conflict becomes worse and leads to a climax.

3. **Climax:** the turning point, or emotional high point for the character(s) in the story. The climax is the most intense moment of the story—where action reaches its peak.

4. **Falling action:** the events that occur after the climax. During the falling action, the events show how the conflict will be resolved.

5. **Resolution:** the consequences or results of the conflict.

Work with a partner. In your notebook, draw a diagram like the one below, which shows plot structure. Write in note form what happens in each part of the story and identify the lines in which the events occur.

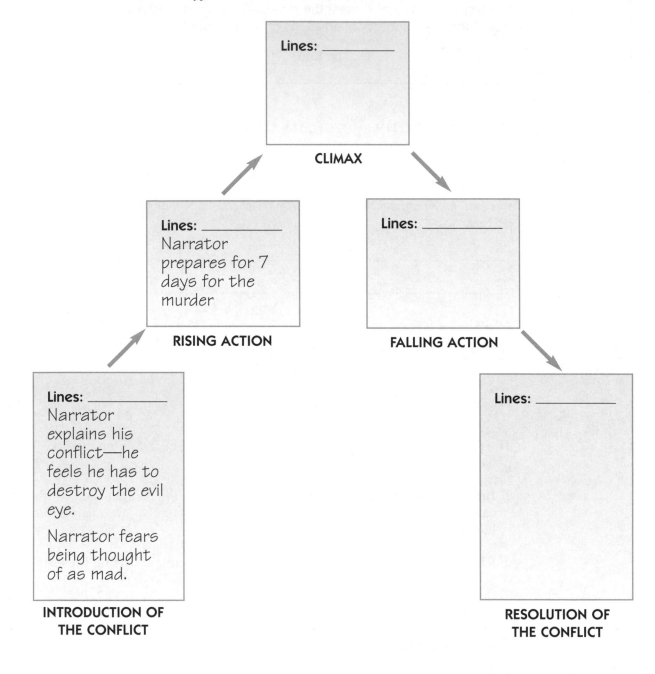

CLIMAX
Lines: _____

RISING ACTION
Lines: _____
Narrator prepares for 7 days for the murder

FALLING ACTION
Lines: _____

INTRODUCTION OF THE CONFLICT
Lines: _____
Narrator explains his conflict—he feels he has to destroy the evil eye.

Narrator fears being thought of as mad.

RESOLUTION OF THE CONFLICT
Lines: _____

With a partner discuss how Poe builds up **suspense** *(the feeling of tension, excitement) before, during, and after the murder.*

C. Evaluating the Narrative Point of View

Point of view refers to who tells the story. When a character tells the story, the point of view is **first person,** and the pronoun *I* is used. When the story is told by the author or narrator who is not a character in the story, the point of view is **third person**.

Contrast the first-person point of view that Poe uses in "The Tell-Tale Heart" with the third-person point of view. Then discuss the questions that follow with a partner.

FIRST-PERSON POINT OF VIEW	THIRD-PERSON POINT OF VIEW
True!—nervous—very, very dreadfully nervous **I** had been and am; but why *will* you say that **I am mad?**	**The young man** had been and is very dreadfully nervous. But why, **he** wonders, do people say **he is mad?**

1. Why did Poe have the main character tell the story of his murder plot? Would it be as interesting from a different point of view?

2. The reader witnesses the murder plot but can't stop it. Why does Poe want the reader to know everything the narrator is thinking?

D. Point-of-View Writing

Choose one of these points of view and write at least one paragraph.

a. Retell this story from the point of view of one of the policemen.

b. Retell this story from the point of view of a psychiatrist who is analyzing the madness of the narrator.

E. Open for Discussion

Discuss these questions in a small group.

1. Does the narrator have any pity for his victim? Does this make the story more or less frightening?

2. Why, in the last scene, does the narrator speak louder and louder?

3. The narrator asks the policemen to "stop dissembling." Do you think that the policemen really are dissembling (pretending)? Do they know the truth? Who is really dissembling in this scene?

4. What do the heartbeats symbolize in this story?

5. Why did the narrator confess to the murder?

IV ▸ Structured Writing Focus

> Write a five-paragraph interpretive essay showing how three of the elements of fiction—plot, narrative point of view, characters, setting, pace, mood, foreshadowing, or irony, communicate a theme (idea) about Poe's story "The Tell-Tale Heart."
>
> ALTERNATIVE TASK: Write a three-paragraph reaction essay to this short story telling why you liked or disliked it.

A. Starting to Write

1. Before You Brainstorm

THE ELEMENTS OF FICTION

In addition to the plot and the narrative point of view, the basic elements of a story consist of:

Characters: The people (and sometimes animals) who take part in the events of the story. Characters may be described in many ways, for example, by their actions, personality, beliefs, appearance, and motivation (the reason for their actions or feelings).

Setting: The time and place of the action of the story, including physical descriptions, such as lighting and sound.

Pace: The rhythm of the story. The pace of a story often moves faster as it nears the climax.

Mood: The feeling the writer creates with the setting and pace. The mood can be romantic, suspenseful, terrifying, adventurous, etc.

Foreshadowing: The hints that suggest future events or actions in the story: descriptions, early events, and symbols, such as the evil eye.

Irony: When a resulting situation is the opposite of what was expected. For example, the narrator says he is very relaxed, not frightened, when the police arrive.

Theme: A main idea of the story. A story can have more than one theme, for example, justice, madness, good vs. evil, appearance vs. reality.

Working with a partner, write in the right columns below first on how setting affects mood and then on how pace affects mood.

Setting	Effect on Mood
Lighting "I undid the lantern just so much that a single thin ray fell upon the vulture eye . . . but I found the eye always closed." (36–39)	1. The single small light emphasizes the darkness of the room, making the mood mysterious and terrifying.
Sound "I undid the lantern cautiously (for the hinges creaked)." (35–36) "With a loud yell, I threw open the lantern and leaped into the room. He shrieked once—once only." (125–126)	2. 3.

Pace	Effect on Mood
Slow "I moved [my head] slowly—very, very slowly so that I might not disturb the old man's sleep. . . . I undid the lantern cautiously. . . . And this I did for seven long nights." (30–37) "Upon the eighth night I was more than usually cautious in opening the door. A watch's minute hand moves more quickly than did mine." (47–49)	1. The narrator's slow, careful movements make time move slowly and make the mood dark and suspenseful. 2.
Fast "As the bell sounded the hour, there came a knocking. . . . three officers of the police. . . . I talked more quickly—more forcefully; but the noise steadily increased. . . . I paced the floor to and fro with heavy strides. . . . but the noise steadily increased. Oh God!" (150–197)	3.

The Tell-Tale Heart　195

Working with a partner, find the symbols below in the reading. In the left column, write what the symbol means. In the right column, write what future event the symbol foreshadows. If you need more room, write in your notebook. The first one has been done for you.

Symbol	Future Event Foreshadowed
1. Vulture eye The old man's "vulture eye" is a cataract, which the narrator thinks is an evil eye with a deadly curse.	The vulture eye foreshadows the old man's death. The narrator thinks that the old man's eye is an evil eye. He believes it must be destroyed, and plans to kill him.
2. Death watches	
3. The old man's heartbeat	

IRONY

Working with a partner, complete these sentences with details from "The Tell-Tale Heart" that show irony. Then with a partner, discuss why each action is ironic. How is the outcome different from what you expected? When you have finished, write other examples of irony from the story in your notebook.

1. Although the narrator feels justified in getting rid of the evil eye,

    he himself becomes _evil_____ in doing so.

2. The narrator blames the policemen for dissimulating, but he's the

    one who _____.

3. As he waits to kill the old man, the narrator thinks that he hears the

    old man's heart beating. At the end of the story when the old man is

    dead, the narrator still _____.

One of the main themes of this story is in its title: "The Tell-Tale Heart." What do you think the title means? Share your answer with a partner.

2. Brainstorming

To choose which three elements of fiction to write about or to gather elements for your reaction essay, consider the following questions and ideas.

1. Which part of the story did you like best? **(plot)**

2. How would you describe the characters to someone who has not read the story? **(characters)**

3. What events were the opposite of what you expected? **(irony)**

4. What was the most suspenseful moment in the story? **(climax)**

5. What ideas(s) do you think this story communicates? **(theme)**

6. How would you turn this story into a movie?

   a. What would the house look like? furniture? colors? lighting? **(setting, mood)**

   b. Which actors would you choose? What would the costumes and make-up look like? **(characters, mood)**

   c. Would you use a "voice-over" (remarks spoken in a movie by someone who cannot be seen)? At which times would you use it? **(narrative point of view)**

   d. Which parts of the movie would go slowly? Which parts would go quickly? **(pace)**

   e. What would be your beginning and ending shot? **(irony, setting)**

FOR THE MAIN TASK

Decide which of the three elements of fiction you plan to write about.

What idea or theme is shown by the three elements you have chosen? For example, how do the setting, characters, and foreshadowing show evil in the story? Which element will you write about first? second? last?

FOR THE ALTERNATIVE TASK

Describe your reaction to Poe's story—did you like it or dislike it? If you liked the story, which element do you think Poe used the best? If you didn't like the story, what would you criticize about it?

B. Preparing the First Draft

1. Supporting Your Interpretation

When you write an essay about a work of literature, you are giving your ideas or opinion about it. To make your ideas and opinion convincing to the reader, you must support them with specific **references quoted from the text**.

Compare the interpretations below. Which one of them is more convincing? Why? Write your thoughts below.

INTERPRETATION A	INTERPRETATION B
The narrator's slow and careful movements as he prepares to kill the old man contribute to the suspense of the story. The narrator describes himself poking his head into the room and watching the old man sleep. The reader feels what the narrator feels, yet is powerless to change the course of events.	The narrator's slow and careful movements as he prepares to kill the old man contribute to the suspense of the story. Poe repeats the words "slowly" and "cautiously" when the narrator enters the old man's room to create a feeling of tension (30, 37, 47). The narrator is so tense as he pokes his head into the room and watches the old man sleep that time seems to stand still. That is why the narrator says, "A watch's minute hand moves more quickly than did mine"(48–49). The reader knows what the narrator is going to do, yet is powerless to change the course of events.

_____

_____

_____

_____

_____

_____

When you write essays for the humanities and social sciences, and when you quote text to support your ideas, you must give references for your quotations by noting the appropriate line or page number(s). For books or long texts, page numbers are usually used. However, for plays, poems, and short stories, line numbers are usually used:

That is why the narrator says, "A watch's minute hand moves more quickly than did mine" **(48–49).**

For citations remember to:

End the quotation marks.

Put the line number(s) between parentheses.

Put in the final punctuation.

Read the following student reaction to "The Tell-Tale Heart." Add the line numbers from the story that the quotes refer to. Then in your notebook, write a paragraph with references from the text and line numbers on one element of fiction or your own reaction to the story.

Response to "The Tell-Tale Heart"

I disliked reading "The Tell-Tale Heart" by Edgar Allan Poe because I find it very distasteful to read the details of a maniac's crime. First, we see how the murderer terrorized his victim and laughed at his suffering. The narrator says, "I knew what the old man felt, and pitied him, although I chuckled at heart" _(72–73)_ . The murderer even admits that "the old man's terror must have been extreme" _____. Finally, when the murderer kills his victim, he stifles him with his own mattress. Poe writes, "I dragged him to the floor, and pulled the heavy bed over him" _____. As readers, we are forced to know what the narrator does to the body to hide his crime when he tells us, "I cut off the head and the arms and the legs" _____. Is this a decent kind of story? I find the main character repulsive. Such immoral people should never be the subject of an artistic effort.

2. Writing an Introduction for an Essay Analyzing Literature

The introduction must give enough background information about the story or author to interest the reader. At the same time, the introduction should not have *too* many details. The support for your ideas and citations comes in the body paragraphs, not in the introduction.

Read those two introductions to essays on "The Tell-Tale Heart." Discuss with a partner which one you prefer and why. What is similar and different about them?

Introduction A

"The Tell-Tale Heart" is one of Edgar Allan Poe's best-known short stories. Madness is a common theme in Poe's stories, and in "The Tell-Tale Heart," this great writer reveals the mind of a madman. The more the narrator tries to prove he isn't crazy, the crazier he reveals he is. Studying the mind of Poe's killer interests me. That is why I am going to write about the **main character, the narrative point of view, and the plot.**

Introduction B

Have you ever had chills run up and down your spine? Have you ever thought there was someone sneaking into your room at night? I felt this same terror when I read Edgar Allan Poe's short story "The Tell-Tale Heart" for the first time. The reader feels suspense from every detail of the ugly crime thanks to Poe's expert creation of a frightening **setting** and his skillful use of **foreshadowing**. Then, the **theme** of justice is revealed through the ironic and dramatic ending.

3. Questions to Consider for Your Own Introduction

1. Is my introduction interesting?

2. Do I mention the author and story title?

3. Do I say what the story is about?

4. For the main task: Does my thesis statement tell which elements of fiction I will discuss?

5. For the alternative task: Does my thesis statement tell my emotional reaction to the story?

4. Organizing Your Essay

Study these block diagrams to help you write your essay on the main task or on the alternative task. In your notebook, draw your own diagram and write your notes in each of its sections.

MAIN TASK

INTRODUCTION
Background information about Poe and the story
Thesis statement

BODY ¶ 1
Topic sentence:
First element of fiction
Support the interpretation with references to the text

Transitional sentence ⬍

BODY ¶ 2
Topic sentence:
Second element of fiction
Support and references

Transitional sentence ⬍

BODY ¶ 3
Topic sentence:
Third element of fiction
Support and references

CONCLUSION
Thesis statement restated

ALTERNATIVE TASK

INTRODUCTION
Background information about Poe and the story
Thesis statement

BODY ¶
Support the idea introduced in the thesis statement with explanations and references to the text

CONCLUSION
Thesis statement restated

*Write a **first draft** of your essay. Remember to write in complete sentences and try to use some of the vocabulary and structures that you have practiced in this unit.*

C. Revising the First Draft

When you have finished writing your first draft, read it to a partner.

CHECKLIST FOR REVISING THE FIRST DRAFT

When you listen to your partner's essay and when you discuss your own, keep these questions in mind:

1. Does the introduction give some background information about the author and the story? Are the author's name and the story title spelled correctly?

2. Is the thesis statement clear?

3. For the main task: Does each body paragraph discuss a different element of fiction mentioned in the thesis statement?

4. Does the essay include line numbers from the text and do they work well to support the writer's opinion? Do line numbers appear in the correct form?

5. Is the essay well-organized? Are the transitions between paragraphs logical and effective?

After discussing your essay with a partner, some reorganization may be necessary.

*Now write a **second draft** that includes all of your additions and changes.*

D. Editing the Second Draft

After you have written a second draft, proofread your work for any errors and correct them. These guidelines and exercises should help.

1. Showing Cause and Effect with *such . . . that / so . . . that*

We sometimes show cause and effect with the expressions *such* + noun + *that* or *so* + adjective/adverb + *that*.

such + noun + *that* + sentence

I replaced the boards with **such cleverness**	**that** no human eye could detect anything wrong.
CAUSE	EFFECT

so + adjective + *that* + sentence

I was **so clever** when I replaced the boards	**that** no human eye could detect anything wrong.
CAUSE	EFFECT

so + adverb + *that* + sentence

I replaced the boards **so cleverly**	**that** no human eye could detect anything wrong.
CAUSE	EFFECT

Working with a partner, write sentences using such . . . that / so . . . that *to describe the following cause-and-effect situations in "The Tell-Tale Heart." In two cases more than one answer is possible.*

1. The narrator feels a lot of anxiety when he looks at the vulture eye.   He knows he must destroy it.

   The narrator feels such anxiety when he looks at the vulture

   eye that he knows he must destroy it.

2. The narrator's sense of hearing is very acute.   He hears all things in heaven and hell.

   The narrator's sense of hearing is so acute that he hears

   all things in heaven and hell.

3. The narrator opens the door to the old man's room very carefully.   The old man doesn't wake up.

   The narrator opens the door to the old man's room so

   carefully that the old man doesn't wake up.

4. The narrator plots his murder with of a lot of secrecy.

The old man doesn't suspect him of the murder plot.

_____

_____

5. The windows are shut very tightly.

No light can enter the old man's room.

_____

_____

6. The narrator listens to the old man's groan with a lot of sympathy.

The act of murder is even more shocking to the reader.

_____

_____

7. The narrator becomes very angry when he sees the vulture eye wide open.

He cannot control himself any more.

_____

_____

8. The narrator believes he appears very relaxed when the policemen enter the house.

He doesn't think they could possibly suspect him.

_____

_____

9. The narrator hears a heart beating very loudly and quickly.

He thinks the policemen hear it too.

_____

_____

2. Simple Present and Simple Past Verbs in an Essay on Literature

THE SIMPLE PRESENT

When you write about any element of fiction or discuss an author's techniques, write in the **simple present.** This is true for any discussion of a work of art (a painting, play, film, etc.).

The narrator **is** friendly to the old man a week before he **murders** him.

SIMPLE PRESENT   SIMPLE PRESENT

THE SIMPLE PAST AND THE SIMPLE PRESENT

When you refer to events in the author's life, use the simple past or whatever other tense is appropriate. If you discuss the author and his or her work *together*, make sure to discuss the work in the simple present.

Poe **wrote** many tales after he **completed** "The Tell-Tale Heart,"

SIMPLE PAST   SIMPLE PAST

but this story, which **relates** to his life, **is** one of his best.

SIMPLE PRESENT   SIMPLE PRESENT

PRACTICE USING THE CORRECT VERB TENSE

Complete these two paragraphs by writing the simple present or the simple past form of the verbs in parentheses. Compare your answers with a partner's.

The events in our lives _____have_____ (have) a
1

great influence on us, and the same

_____ (be) true for writers, including
2

Edgar Allan Poe. Poe _____
3

(become) an orphan when he _____
4

(be) two years old. He_____
5

(not / have) a good relationship with his

foster father, John Allan. Today, some literary

critics _____ (suggest) that the old man in
6

"The Tell-Tale Heart," with his evil eye, _____ (be) the image of
7

Poe's foster father.

The heart beat in the story also _____ (have) a connection with
8

Poe's life. Everyone knows the famous scene where the narrator

_____ (hear) the beating of his victim's heart and _____ (lose)
9   10

his control in front of the policemen. In the summer of 1842, Poe

_____ (have) a severe heart attack. Because he had a near-death
11

experience, we _____ (understand) why the heartbeat _____
12   13

(play) such an important role in "The Tell-Tale Heart," which Poe

_____ (write) the following year.
14

E. Preparing the Final Draft

Reread your second draft and correct any errors you find. Put a check (✓) in each
space as you edit for these points. Then write your corrected final version.

> ### CHECKLIST FOR EDITING THE SECOND DRAFT
>
> _____ cause and effect with *such . . . that / so . . . that*
>
> _____ simple present and simple past verbs in an essay
> on literature

Additional Writing Opportunities

Write about one of the following topics.

1. "Shrinklit" (shrinking literature) poems are jokes that shorten the plot of a work of literature and make it funny. This is one about "The Tell-Tale Heart." It is inspired by a book called *Shrinklits* by Maurice Sagoff.

   THE TELL-TALE HEART
   by Dipika Chawla

   An insane, crazy guy,
   strangely vexed by a vulture eye.

   He's not crazy—he says with might,
   reader answers, "Oh, yeah, right!"

   Gonna kill that oldie guy,
   does it being shrewd and sly.

   Eighth night does the awful deed,
   under floorboards with great ease.

   Cops come in—they hear a shriek,
   find nothing when they take a peek.

   Then he hears a ghost heartbeat,
   cannot stay atop his seat.

   Admits the murder—what a sting,
   guilt can be an awful thing!

   Write an essay on whether you think this shrinklit summarizes the plot of "The Tell-Tale Heart" well? Why or why not?

2. Read another short story written by Edgar Allan Poe and write an analysis of it. Explain how three elements of fiction show a theme or mood in the story. Some recommendations are "The Murders in the Rue Morgue," and "The Gold-Bug." You may also want to look at easier adapted versions of Poe stories found in *Tales of Mystery and Imagination* by Edgar Allan Poe (Oxford University Press © 2000).

3. Some critics have said that Poe's dark writing was influenced by his sad and tortured life. Research Poe's biography at the library or on the Internet. Then, write a five-paragraph essay about whether you think his life experiences influenced his writing. If so, how? Remember to support your ideas with facts from his life and references and citations from "The Tell-Tale Heart."

SUPPLEMENTARY ACTIVITIES

These suggestions come from our own classes and the classes of our colleagues.

UNIT 1
PATHWAY TO FREEDOM

Films for Listening and Discussion

1. Show students any of the films listed below. You may want to divide the film into sections to watch over a couple or a few class sessions or show only parts of it. Before the film, give a short introduction to the topic. Then after students watch the film, have them answer general comprehension questions in a small group.

- *Glory* (1989), starring Denzel Washington and Morgan Freeman, is a film about the regiments of black soldiers who fought for their freedom in the American Civil War. Frederick Douglass lobbied President Lincoln to create these regiments and sent his son to fight in one of them. Some of the film content is very violent, but historically accurate.
- *The Civil War* (1991) is a documentary by Ken Burns. One excerpt of special interest is "All Night Forever" from the first tape in the series, Episode 1: "1861, The Cause", which shows archive photographs of life under slavery.
- *The Long Walk Home* (1990), starring Whoopi Goldberg and Sissy Spacek, is a film about the Montgomery Bus Boycott. This was a boycott against segregated buses in the South that launched the Civil Rights movement of the 1950s and the career of Martin Luther King, Jr.

Listening and Summarizing

2. Have students read excerpts from Martin Luther King Jr.'s "I have a dream" speech. Then play a video or audiotape of the speech while students take notes. Afterward, have students write a summary of the main ideas of his dream.

Internet Research

3. Have students research and report on the role the following people played in the Civil War and the abolitionist movement against slavery: Frederick Douglass, Harriet Tubman, Sojourner Truth, Nat Turner, and John Brown. After students give their reports, divide them into groups to discuss and compare the biographies. What are the differences between these people's points of view and actions? How did each contribute to the end of slavery? Which of the people do the students identify with or admire most and why?

UNIT 2
WHAT'S YOUR VERDICT?

Films for Listening and Discussion

1. Show students *Twelve Angry Men* (1957), a black and white film about the American jury system. Divide the film into sections to be seen over a couple or a few class sessions. Hold a discussion after each section of the film that you show. Ask students to identify the backgrounds and prejudices of the jury. Would there be many all-white juries today? What is a verdict "beyond a reasonable doubt"? How does one juror convince the others? What does this film tell us about democracy and responsibility?

Mock Trial

2. Stage a mock trial of Leroy Strachan to develop students' speaking fluency. Ask students to play roles (Strachan, the prosecuting and defense attorneys, the judge, the witnesses, and the jury). For a small class, the jury may be composed of fewer than six people. After the trial, have students discuss their performance and the difficulties they encountered with vocabulary, grammar, and pronunciation. Give students feedback in the form of a short list of common errors and discuss it as a class, or write individual feedback for students on cards. This is easier if the trial is audiotaped or videotaped. You can comment on fluency, word choice, sentence structure, or pronunciation.

Internet Research

3. Have students research either one of these topics using the Internet:

- *Brown v. Board of Education:* the Supreme Court case on the desegregation of American public schools
- U.S. prisons: their purpose, population, construction, supervision; criticism of prisons and proposals for their reform.

Have students write reports based on their research, report on their topics to the class, or audiotape themselves and exchange tapes with a partner.

UNIT 3
MEN AND WOMEN: NOTHING BUT THE FACTS

Reading Comprehension

1. Have students read about the division of labor in the home among American couples. Then have students comment on their findings. What conditions encourage more equality in the home? One good source to recommend is the book *The Second Shift*, by Arlie Hochschild, a landmark study of the unequal roles of men and women in the home.

Internet Research

2. Divide students into groups so that some research women's rights, including suffrage (the right to vote) in the United States, while other groups research women's rights in another country of their choice. Have students research their topic on the Internet and present their findings to another group. Give the groups some research questions such as the following: When did the women's suffrage movement begin in the United States and what were its aims? What opposition did the movement encounter? What is the status of women's right to vote in the country you have chosen? How is the social status of these women similar to or different from the social status of women in the United States?

Ask students to take notes during the other group presentations. Then, ask each student to write a paragraph comparing and contrasting women's rights in two of the countries from the presentation, using the comparison language from this unit.

UNIT 4
THE BEST TIME TO BE ALIVE

Using Maps for Context

1. Have students work in pairs to locate on a world map where the societies from the reading are located. This will give students more context for better reading comprehension. Next show the class how to draw a timeline. Have pairs of students draw a timeline that includes all of the historical periods from the reading.

Films for a Listening Cloze and Discussion

2. Show segments from any of the science fiction films discussed in the unit: *Fahrenheit 451* (1966), *Soylent Green* (1973), *Gattaca* (1997), or *Metropolis* (1927).

For intensive listening practice, give students a cloze (a paragraph to a page) of a short listening segment from the film. Play the film segment several times while students fill in the blanks. Then work on vocabulary enrichment.

For general understanding, have students answer discussion questions about longer segments of the film: What is the film's vision of the future? What impression does the film make on the viewer?

Art Museum / Art Exhibition

3. Take the class to an art museum. Have students write notes on objects of art from one particular society. Ask students to write a description of the art, including an introduction about the society it is from, which they may research using the Internet.

If there is no art museum in your area, or if an outing is not possible, have students bring in traditional arts, audio recordings, costumes, textiles, crafts, or games from their countries or cultures. Ask them to explain the background, use, or symbolism of their objects while the other students take notes on the presentations and write a brief summary.

Internet Research

4. Have students research the history of their country of origin, or a country of their choice. Have students look up statistical information on the country using an almanac, encyclopedia, or factbook, available on the Internet. Then ask students to write several descriptive paragraphs about the country, including details such as its form of government, languages spoken, religions, history, or recent politics.

UNIT 5
THE HAPPIEST SCHOOL IN THE WORLD

Oral reports

1. Put students in groups and ask them to report on their educational background. What were the positive and negative aspects of their education? What would they change if they could? Have group members take notes during each report. Then have students write several paragraphs comparing their own educational experience to that of another student. What are the similarities or differences between their experiences?

Debate

2. Should schoolteachers ever use physical discipline on children or teenagers? How can young people develop self-discipline? Brainstorm in class to compare experiences and gather information, arguments, and reasons.

Natural History Museum

3. Take your class to a natural history museum. Divide students into groups and have them categorize museum objects into one category such as gems and minerals, birds, mammals, or stars. Have students take notes in order to write a summary of their category. If students need more assistance, discuss their categories as a class.

Internet Research

4. Have students research the history of Montessori schools: the life of Maria Montessori in Italy, how she developed her method, how Montessori schools differ from ordinary schools. For additional options, have students research Rudolph Steiner, founder of the Waldorf schools, or John Dewey, the well-known U.S. educator.

UNIT 6
ARE YOU GETTING ENOUGH SLEEP?

Journal Writing

1. Ask students to record their sleeping and waking patterns for a week and comment on them with a partner or in a small group. They can graph the results and discuss them. You might also have them record their dreams and comment on them with other students.

Internet Research

2. Have students use the Internet to research how to get a good night's sleep. Ask each student to write a letter to a partner complaining about real or imagined sleep problems. Then have students answer the letter from their partner using the research they found.

UNIT 7
HOW I'LL BECOME AN AMERICAN

Using Films for Listening, Writing, and Acting

1. Show students scenes from a film or TV show that uses silent comedy. For example, *The Immigrant* or *Goldrush* by Charlie Chaplin, or episodes from *I Love Lucy*. Especially recommended is Episode 39, "Job Switching," the famous episode where Lucy gets a job packaging chocolates on a conveyor belt, and ends up eating most of them. After the viewing, ask students to write their version of the (unspoken) dialogue, retell the story, describe the characters, and explain what is funny about the scene. They can also act out the scenes in small groups, adding their own improvisations if they wish.

Satirical Comics

2. Have students draw and caption satirical comics like the ones on pages 119 and 126. They might want to draw one on what life in the United States is like for someone new to this country. Their series of sketches can be reproduced as a class book.

Internet Research

3. Have the students research and report on the biography of Charlie Chaplin, Jim Carey, or another humorous film actor, writer, stand-up comic, circus clown, or cartoonist, such as "Peanuts" creator, Charles Schultz. What leads people to become humorists? Is it true that people who become humorists or humorous actors have often had sad lives? What qualities are needed to be a good comic actor? cartoonist? comic writer?

UNIT 8
FOR AND AGAINST BILINGUAL EDUCATION

Suggested Topics for Internet Research

1. Have students research immigration to a country other than the United States, such as Germany, France, Denmark, Canada, or Australia. How are immigrants treated in the country? Why do people immigrate there? Do they find many opportunities? Can they become citizens? Do they speak their own language or must they learn the language of the country? What obstacles do they face? How do these countries compare to the United States in terms of their policies and attitudes toward immigrants?

2. Ask students to work in pairs or small groups to research bilingualism in a country other than the United States, such as Canada, where Quebec is a French-speaking province within a large English-speaking country, or in Belgium, which has French-speaking and Flemish-speaking regions, or Switzerland, which has four official languages. Students can add other countries of their choice. Why would the country have two or more official languages? What are the government policies regarding this issue and what problems, if any, have resulted from bilingualism?

UNIT 9
CASE STUDIES IN BUSINESS ETHICS

Project: Create Your Own Business

1. Have students work in pairs or groups to create a business. First, brainstorm a list of questions with the class that the groups might consider: Would they offer goods or a service? Where would they get the start-up money? Where would they locate? How would they advertise and attract customers? After a group discussion, and research if necessary, have the groups explain their ideas in an oral presentation. Then ask the other students listening to write which group they would invest in and why.

Make Your Own Commercial

2. Have students work in small groups to create an interesting or humorous commercial for a product or service they have invented. First give the students time to plan their commercial. Then have them perform it on audiotape or videotape, asking the class to vote on or write about the best product or service.

Suggested Topics for Internet Research

3. Assign students to research different business schools, such as Harvard, Wharton at the University of Pennsylvania, or local business schools. Tell students to look at the school Web-sites and write notes on the courses, degrees, costs, and job opportunities that they offer or promise. Then have

students write a few paragraphs on their research. Is it important to attend business school to succeed in business? Why or why not? What is taught in these schools? Which school would they most like to attend and why?

UNIT 10
THE TELL-TALE HEART

Using Authentic Recordings for Listening

1. Play students an audio-tape of a professional reading of the "The Tell-Tale Heart" to increase their enjoyment of the text and to link listening with reading.

Mock Trial

2. Have students stage an imaginary trial of the narrator from "The Tell-Tale Heart," playing the roles of the narrator (the accused), the old man (the witness), two attorneys, a judge, and the jury. Give students time to write out their arguments and testimony. Encourage them to enact the trial on videotape, which they may watch later. Have students vote at the end of the trial whether they believe that the narrator should be punished for his murder, and what the punishment should be, or if the narrator should be found innocent by reason of insanity and committed to a psychiatric institution.

Reading

3. Read Poe's poems "Annabel Lee" or "The Raven" (divided in parts) to students. Begin by pre-teaching difficult vocabulary items. Read the poem again for the students so that they hear it more than once. Then give them general comprehension questions to write or discuss.

Internet Research

4. Divide the class into groups, or if the class is small let them work individually, and have them research a different aspect of Edgar Allan Poe's life and work. Have them use the Internet and books at the library. Then ask students to report to the class on the topic they have chosen. Some suggested topics are Poe's relationship with his stepfather, John Allan, his marriage with Virginia Clemm, his unconventional life, and his mysterious death.

ANSWER KEY

UNIT 1
THE PATHWAY TO FREEDOM

II. Reading for Writing
A. General Understanding (p. 4)

1. d, e   2. i   3. f
4. a   5. g, h

1. (Answers will vary.) Douglass began his story by talking about his family to introduce the reader to his background and to show what an unfair and difficult life his mother had.
2. At first Mrs. Auld was very kind and started to teach Douglass how to read. However, when her husband told her not to teach him, she became violently opposed to his learning to read.
3. Douglass saw no reason to live without the hope of being free.
4. Douglass changed his mind when he read a newspaper article about people from the North praying for the end of slavery, and decided to run away.

In the second paragraph, Douglass finds the pathway to freedom through reading. The slave system corrupts even the kindest person.

In the third paragraph, Douglass learns to read from children and realizes the injustice of slavery.

In the fourth paragraph, Douglass's hatred toward his enslavers grows. He gains a new hope of being free.

B. Working with Language (p. 5)
1. Adjectives Describing Behavior

1. obedient   7. generous
2. practical   8. manipulative
3. fearful   9. courageous
4. childish   10. foolish
5. sympathetic   11. helpless
6. clever   12. cruel

2. Describing Characters
(Answers will vary.)
1. helpless, obedient
2. cruel, fearful, foolish, obedient
3. cruel, manipulative
4. courageous, clever, practical, helpless, generous
5. sympathetic, practical

3. Identifying Nouns and Adjectives

2. clever   7. foolish
3. practical   8. obedient
4. courage   9. manipulation
5. cruel   10. fear
6. sympathy

IV. Structured Writing Focus
B. Preparing the First Draft (p. 12)
Choosing Ideas for Paragraph Unity

1. The main idea of the paragraph is why the writer decided that business was a good career for her.
2. The following two sentences do not support the main idea: On the weekends I slept in; Unfortunately, a business slump has caused many store closings in our area.

D. Editing the Second Draft (p. 15)
1. Habitual Past vs. Simple Past

1. b, c   2. a   3. c

1. used to be, were
2. used to go, went
3. used to learn, learned
4. started
5. decided
6. realized

2. Avoiding Repetition: Pronouns and Possessive Adjectives

1. Very little communication ever took place between my mother and me. <u>She</u> died when I was seven years old. I was not allowed to be present during <u>her</u> illness, at <u>her</u> death, or at <u>her</u> burial. <u>She</u> was gone before I knew anything about it.
2. I have had two masters. My first master's last name was Anthony. I do not remember <u>his</u> first name. <u>He</u> was not considered a rich slaveholder. <u>He</u> owned two or three farms and about thirty slaves.
3. Mr. and Mrs. Auld were both at home, and <u>they</u> met me at the door with <u>their</u> little son, Thomas.

3. Style Rules
Frederick Douglass, an American Hero

<u>Frederick Douglass</u> played an extraordinary role in <u>American</u> history. He was born a slave in <u>Maryland</u> in 1817. <u>He</u> never saw his brother and two sisters until he was seven years old. He later wrote in his *Narrative*, <u>"Slavery made us strangers."</u> At 21, Douglass worked on the docks in Baltimore. <u>From</u>

there, he managed to escape from slavery using the identity papers of a free black sailor. He then went to <u>New York City</u>, where he married <u>Ann Murray</u>, a free black woman whom he had first met in <u>Baltimore</u>. <u>He</u> chose a new name: <u>Douglass</u>, from Sir Walter Scott's novel, *The Lady of the Lake*. <u>In</u> his new life, <u>Frederick</u> <u>Douglass</u> became an important abolitionist. <u>He</u> helped slaves escape to the <u>North</u> by means of the Underground Railroad. <u>In</u> 1847, he began to publish his own newspaper called *The North Star*. This was the name of the star that escaping slaves followed north in search of freedom. In his newspaper, <u>Douglass</u> fought for justice for the oppressed. <u>At</u> the first Women's Rights Convention in 1848, he demanded that women be allowed to vote. During the <u>Civil War</u>, he pressured <u>President Lincoln</u> to allow black people to fight in the Union Army for their freedom. Douglass's sons fought among the black troops. Douglass later became <u>U.S.</u> ambassador to <u>Haiti</u>, the world's first black republic. He also became a leader of <u>Howard University</u>, the first university for African Americans in the United States. Frederick Douglass is an American hero.

UNIT 2
WHAT'S YOUR VERDICT?

II. Reading for Writing

A. General Understanding (p. 23)

(Answers will vary.)

2. A police officer was killed by a single rifle shot.
3. John Milledge is the name of the police officer that was killed.
4. A Miami woman who saw the crime take place went to the police 45 years after the event to accuse Leroy Strachan of the crime.
5. William Kunstler is Leroy Strachan's attorney.
6. Florida is the state where the crime took place.
7. New York is the state where Leroy Strachan was arrested.

B. Working with Language (p. 24)

1. Learning Legal Vocabulary

2. c   3. b   4. d   5. f   6. e

1. defense attorney   6. witnesses
2. prosecutor   7. verdict
3. judge   8. unanimous
4. jury   9. defendant
5. evidence   10. sentence

2. Reading the U.S. Constitution

2. a   3. f   4. b   5. h   6. i
7. c   8. g   9. e

III. Prewriting Activities

A. Constitutional or Unconstitutional? (p. 27)

1. Unconstitutional—The man did not know why he was arrested. He never saw a lawyer.
2. Unconstitutional—The jury was not impartial.
3. Unconstitutional—The trial was not in the state where the crime was committed. There was no mention of witnesses either.
4. Constitutional

IV. Structured Writing Focus

B. Preparing the First Draft (p. 30)

1. Essay Structure: Writing Introductions, Body Paragraphs, and Conclusions

1. The ideas proceed from general to specific.
2. The purpose of the body paragraph is to give support for the thesis statement.
3. The conclusion reminds the reader of the main idea in the introduction.

2. The Introduction and the Thesis Statement

More specific ideas

"We are not alone in this world, and what we do has an effect on others. In fact, what we do for prisoners will affect our lives as well as theirs."

Most specific idea

"If we want criminals to become useful members of society when they get out of jail, we must educate them while they are still in prison."

3. The Body

2. We should offer a basic skills program to prisoners who want to change.
3. We should give prisoners up-to-date job training.

4. We should give prisoners psychological counseling and religious or moral instruction.

4. The Conclusion

1. Prisoners can become better future citizens, but we must educate them while they are still in prison to make their reform a success.

2. We will not only improve their lives, we will ensure the safety of our society.

5. Practice with introductions, Thesis Statements, Body Support, and Conclusions

Organizing an Introduction

Logical order of sentences for introduction:

1. We are all members of society.

2. When we do something that harms society, we have to be punished.

3. This punishment usually takes the form of a prison sentence.

4. However, it is very expensive to house and feed prisoners.

5. It would be unreasonable to burden society with the added expense of providing prisoners with a free education.

Evaluating thesis Statements

5. T   6. F   7. I   8. T

Supporting a thesis Statement

Good Support: 3, 4, 6

Choosing the best conclusion

Conclusion B is not a good conclusion for this essay because it goes off the topic after the first sentence and discusses crime in general. The main ideas of the essay are not mentioned here. Conclusion A is a good conclusion because it restates the idea that prison should be a punishment.

D. Editing the Second Draft (p. 35)

1. Active and Passive Voice

2. The defendant was questioned by both lawyers.

3. The whole process is being supervised by the judge.

4. During a trial, the defendant will be confronted by all of the witnesses.

5. All of the testimony has been heard by the jury.

6. By the end of the day, a verdict had been reached by the jury.

3. determines

4. kills

5. is recommended

6. is understood

7. is expected

8. is called

9. is not punished

10. he committed

11. is recommended

12. is thought

2. Transitive and Intransitive Verbs

2. has risen	6. now exists
3. ✓	7. ✓
4. has grown	8. has occurred
5. remain	

UNIT 3

MEN AND WOMEN: NOTHING BUT THE FACTS

II. Reading for Writing

A. General Understanding (p. 43)

1. What Do the Statistics Say?

1. F   2. T   3. F

4. T   5. T   6. T

2. What Proof Do You Have?

(Answers will vary.)

1. 52 percent of the girls and 59 percent of the boys believe there is no difference between being a boy or a girl.

2. 58 percent of the boys expect their wives to work; however, 86 percent of the girls expect to work after they get married.

3. Like most of the girls, most of the boys agree they want children. 92 percent of the girls and 94 percent of the boys expect to have children.

4. 34 percent of girls say that boys think girls and boys are equal. However, 63% of girls say that boys think girls are inferior to boys.

5. 77 percent of the girls said they would still be happy if they got divorced, while 22 percent of the girls would not be happy if they got divorced.

3. What Conclusions Can You Reach?

1. No   2. No   3. No

4. No   5. Yes   6. Yes

4. Converting Statistics from a Paragraph to a Graph

Women and Men in Managerial Positions
Women: 46.7%, Men: 53.3%

Women and Men as Lawyers
Women: 33%, Men: 67%

Women and Men as Judges
Women: 27.5%, Men: 72.5%

B. Working with Language (p. 46)

The Gender Gap

2. quickly/steadily/sharply/steeply
3. go up/rise/increase
4. gradually/slowly/slightly
5. sharp/steep
6. increase/growth/rise
7. slight
8. increase/growth/rise
9. rose/went up/increased/grew
10. declined/fell/went down/
    decreased

IV. Structured Writing Focus

A. Starting to Write (p. 50)

Brainstorming

Table A
1. F   2. F   3. T
Table B
1. F   2. T   3. F
Table C
1. T   2. F   3. T

B. Preparing the First Draft (p. 51)

1. Analyzing Essay Structure

1. In most countries women have not achieved complete equality in the workplace.
2. The statistics support the main idea that women do not earn wages that are equal to men's by showing the following: In 1990, women still earned only 50% of men's wages in Japan; in the U.S., women made 70% of men's wages; and even in Europe, women's wages were 90% of men's.
3. Conclusion: The gender wage gap exists but is slowly getting smaller. Sweden is the leader in giving women wages that are almost equal to men's.

D. Editing the Second Draft (p. 53)

1. Contrasting Verb Tenses

2. provide   8. did not earn

3. have entered   9. increased
4. has grown   10. were
5. were   11. received
6. were   12. have made
7. did

2. Subject-Verb Agreement

2. ✓   3. is   4. ✓
5. was   6. ✓

UNIT 4
THE BEST TIME TO BE ALIVE

II. Reading for Writing

A. General Understanding (p. 61)

1. China
2. China, Japan, Nigeria, U.S.A.
3. Japan, Nigeria
4. U.S.A.
5. China, Japan
6. Japan

1. (*Answers will vary.*) Russell Baker might have explained that the present is not the best time to live because our world is experiencing international terrorism, a deadly AIDS epidemic, and ethnic wars in areas such as Bosnia.
2. When Jonathan Spence describes the Ming dynasty as "a rich time to live," he does not mean rich in terms of money. He means it was a sophisticated and cultured time. Literature played a big role in people's lives; so did art and good food.
3. Orlando Patterson is attracted to the rebellious lifestyle of the merchants in Tokugawa Japan, who liked to disobey the shogun. He is also interested in Kabuki theater and mentions that it was a peaceful time, when a person could have a long life.
4. Orlando Patterson chose 14th-century Ife as his ideal time to live because of the beautiful art created during this period.
5. (*Answers will vary.*) If Ann Douglas were a man, she might have chosen 19th-century America as the best time to live because she would have been able to play a part in the abolitionist movement, and she would have had more freedom as a woman in that society.
6. Elaine Pagels would disagree that life was better in the past, because in the past many children died due to poor medical care. Also, in the past people were less aware of other cultures, whereas now, with global

communication and technological progress, people are "less closed off" from the rest of the world.

B. Working with Language (p. 62)

2. sophisticated
3. prosperous
4. privileged
5. bureaucrats
6. determined
7. economic
8. incredible

III. Prewriting Activities

B. Science Fiction (p. 63)

(Answers will vary.)

1. The book warns us about the danger of mindless TV programs replacing books.
2. The film warns us what can happen if we don't take care of the environment.
3. The film warns us about possible consequences of genetic engineering.

IV. Structured Writing Focus

B. Preparing the First Draft (p. 66)

1. Analyzing Essay Structure
Student essay first draft
a. Introduction
b. Body paragraph 1
c. Body paragraph 2
d. Body paragraph 3
e. Conclusion
(Answers will vary.)

1. Ever since the writer was in junior high school, she has been interested in history and has wondered about what life would have been like in the past. The writer could get the reader's attention with an example of a period that she found exciting.
2. "Peace, a chance for women, and the love of my family and friends are the reasons why I would choose to live my life at the present time." The thesis could be stated more directly.
3. No, the paragraphs do not follow the order of the ideas in the thesis statement. The paragraph on "peace" should come before the paragraph on "a chance for women."
4. Specific historical examples could be added to give more support to the body paragraph on peace.
5. The conclusion is one simple sentence. This is not enough for a paragraph. To develop the conclusion, the writer can

connect the three topics to her own personal experience and to the passage of time.
Student essay second draft

1. Yes. The writer included an example of a past time period that interested her.
2. Yes. The body paragraphs follow the order of the ideas in the thesis statement.
3. In the second draft, the body paragraph on peace offers specific historical details. For example, it compares our time to past generations that experienced world wars. The paragraph also discusses the current global interest in making the world more peaceful.
4. Yes. The writer effectively summarizes her three main ideas and makes a powerful statement about her hope to lead a meaningful life in the present and future.

2. The Thesis Statement: Creating Unity

3. Yes. The writer will show how we will live and think differently in the future because of three causes: the development of technology, the spread of democracy, and the discoveries of medicine.
4. No. While this *is* an opinion, we do not know how (i.e., in what ways) the future will be a utopia.
5. Yes. The writer will show three ways life in the past was more human: it was less stressful, less cruel, and more compatible with nature.
6. No. We know the topic, but not the period of time the writer is going to write about or the reason that this time is perfect.
7. Yes. The writer will discuss how we cannot recapture the past despite our efforts in three areas: research, scholarship, and imagination.

4. Paragraph Order: Creating Coherence
The student essay uses the order "from least personal to most personal."

5. Choosing the Best Conclusion
Conclusion A is better because the writer restates every idea from the thesis statement that was developed in the body paragraphs. In Conclusion B, the writer adds a different topic that was not discussed in the essay: getting an

education from books. A new topic should never be introduced in the conclusion.

D. Editing the Second Draft (p. 72)

1. Adjective Clauses

2. Metropolis, the city of the future, has an underground prison city where workers live and work. Metropolis, the city of the future, has an underground prison city that/which workers live and work in.

3. The Masters of Metropolis rule the machines that/which control the workers.

4. This was an age of cruelty when people were suffering.

5. The son of one of the Masters falls in love with a worker girl who/that helps the workers to revolt against the Masters.

6. Fritz Lang was the great film director who/that directed *Metropolis*.

2. Present Unreal Conditionals

1. are	4. would not suffer
2. were	5. lived
3. would have	6. would want

UNIT 5
THE HAPPIEST SCHOOL IN THE WORLD

II. Reading for Writing

A. General Understanding (p. 80)

1. What Happens at Summerhill?

1. Yes. No one tells the students what to wear. They can wear whatever they want.

2. No. Punishments are not decided by teachers alone. Teachers and students have equal votes.

3. Yes. Students decide for themselves which classes they want to take.

4. Yes. A student could choose to go to class one day a week; however, the other students might ask that student to leave for impeding their progress.

5. No. No attention is paid to such things as handwriting.

6. No. Although creativity and originality are encouraged, no one has to study music or anything else.

7. No. The students live at the school.

8. No. There are no special teaching methods at the school. If students want to learn, they will.

2. The Main Idea and Your Response
(Answers will vary.)

In the reading A. S. Neill talks about a unique school called Summerhill, where students have complete freedom to live and learn as they wish. He criticizes traditional schools by saying that they prevent creativity and originality in students and that they oppress children.

B. Working with Language (p. 81)

1. Describing Summerhill and Ordinary Schools

Ordinary Schools: conformist, docile, fights, obedient, quarrel, robots

Summerhill: creative, free, loaf, playful

2. The Author's Purpose: Criticizing Ordinary Schools and Society
(Answers will vary.)

Summerhill challenges the materialism of society. Instead of teaching children to be robots, Summerhill teaches them to be creative, thinking individuals.

Summerhill challenges the assumption that adults such as parents and educators should make all the decisions for a child. Summerhill gives children many rights, such as a vote at the General School Meeting.

3. Finding Synonyms

2. forbidden	5. downtrodden
3. required, obligated	6. by choice
4. hinder, block	7. harsh

4. The Principles of Summerhill

2. compelled	5. impedes
3. severe	6. oppressed
4. banned	

III. Prewriting Activities

A. The U.S. Educational System (p. 83)

1. Elementary/primary school: age 6; middle school: age 10; 4-year high school: age 14

2. Senior high school diploma: 3 years

3. Bachelor's degree: 4 years; master's degree: 2 years

4. M.A.; Ph.D.; professional degrees in law, medicine, theology, etc.

B. Interpreting Quotes (p. 84)

(Answers will vary.)

2. Students learn the most from each other, not from the teacher.

3. In order to be free, a person has to be educated.

4. Encouragement is the most important element of education.

5. If you teach a child well when he is young, this education will stay with him all his life.

6. Education will protect freedom better than an army.

7. Universities teach too many subjects and too much information that is not important to know.

8. To teach a person in secular subjects like philosophy, math, and science, without teaching him morals, makes him a danger to society.

C. Classification (p. 84)

Freedom: 3, 6

Meaning: 2, 4, 7

Morality: 5, 8

IV. Structured Writing Focus

A. Starting to Write (p. 85)

1. Before You Brainstorm

1. "Golding divides people into three categories: grade-three thinkers, grade-two thinkers, and grade-one thinkers."

2. Body paragraph 1: "According to Golding, 90 percent of the population represents the largest category, called grade-three thinkers."

   Body paragraph 2: "Grade-two thinkers, Golding's second category, are less likely to be influenced by a dictator."

   Body paragraph 3: "The remaining 1 percent of the population are what Golding calls grade-one thinkers."

3. 90 percent: grade-three thinkers, 9 percent: grade-two thinkers, 1 percent: grade-one thinkers

4. Grade-one thinkers see corruption and know how to seek truth. Their lives are defined by wisdom, beauty, and knowledge. Such thinkers are creative and imaginative geniuses, like Mozart, Michelangelo, and Einstein.

5. The writer's opinion appears in the conclusion: The writer disagrees with Golding's belief that highly intelligent people always behave intelligently. He/She shows through historical references how "grade-one thinkers" supported dictators in the way that Golding would have expected his "grade-three thinkers" to behave.

6. To support his point of view, the writer gives examples of doctors, teachers, lawyers, and writers who supported Hitler, Stalin, and Mao.

Establishing a principle of classification

2. ~~private~~
   principle of classification: different school levels

3. ~~experienced~~
   principle of classification: personalities of teachers

4. ~~history~~
   principle of classification: science subjects

5. ~~hard workers~~
   principle of classification: kinds of professions that people have

B. Preparing the First Draft (p. 89)

1. Writing a Thesis Statement for a Classification Essay

(Answers will vary.)

2. There are three types of friends in my life: childhood friends, friends from school, and friends from work.

3. My large family can best be categorized geographically: my family in New York, my family in Miami, and my family in Cuba.

D. Editing the Second Draft (p. 92)

1. Parallel Structure

(Answers will vary.)

1. those who study an average amount
2. to yell
3. watch TV
4. nervous
5. pretend
6. thoughtfully

2. enthusiastic
3. worthless objects
4. artists
5. ✓
6. collecting
7. forgetting

2. Quantifiers: *One of* Many

2. one of the highest grades
3. one of the math awards was
4. one of a good teacher's abilities is
5. ✓
6. one of many people

UNIT 6
ARE YOU GETTING ENOUGH SLEEP?
II. Reading for Writing
A. General Understanding (p. 100)
1. Understanding the Main Idea
1. The main idea of the essay is understanding the importance of sleep and describing the three major causes of sleep deprivation. Thesis statement: "We clearly need to sleep more and educate people about the three major causes of sleep deprivation: modern technology, insomnia, and sleep apnea."
2. Effect of sleep deprivation: car accidents
3. The writer says, "We need to reduce sleep deprivation, which is caused by 24-hour schedules, insomnia, and sleep apnea, because one person's sleepiness can result in the next person's tragedy."

2. Identifying Causes
Social cause: technology
Associated topics: artificial light, shift work
Psychological cause: insomnia
Associated topics: stress at work, family arguments, depression
Physical cause: sleep apnea
Associated topics: snoring, gasping for air

B. Working with Language (p. 101)
1. Crossword Puzzle
Across: 1. risk   5. symptom   6. alert
7. cycle   9. environment   11. essential
12. ignore   13. well-being
Down: 1. restorative   2. function
3. categories   4. awareness
7. complex   8. deprive   10. deep

2. The Two Stages of Sleep
1. deprive   7. deep
2. ignore   8. essential
3. well-being   9. restorative
4. risk   10. environment
5. cycle   11. function
6. alert

IV. Structured Writing Focus
B. Preparing the First Draft (p. 107)
1. Creating Body Paragraphs from Research Notes
1. "Not getting enough sleep can have a negative effect on how well students do in school."
2. "Students are at risk for lower scores on standardized tests due to poor sleep habits," writes Research Psychologist Anna Kroncke. Quoting a specialist, such as a psychologist in this case, makes the writer's argument stronger by showing that it is supported by experts in the field.
3. "According to a National Sleep Foundation Poll, 10 percent of high school students are late at least one day each month because they oversleep." Yes, the statistic supports the idea in the topic sentence.
4. "When I was in high school, I was always tired because I stayed up late talking to my friends. I really needed more time to sleep every morning, but school started early." The writer added a personal experience to give an example of how the statistics and facts he/she is presenting are true.
5. "Their whole school future could suffer because of a lack of sleep." The conclusion reinforces the topic sentence by emphasizing that sleep deprivation can negatively influence students' futures as well as their current schoolwork.

2. Transitional Sentences
The transitional sentence in the second body paragraph is also the topic sentence because it connects ideas between paragraphs and clearly announces the topic.

The transitional sentence in the third body paragraph is not the topic sentence because it does not clearly state the exact topic of that paragraph. It is followed by the topic sentence.

Practice with transitional sentences
Choice a. is a good transition sentence for this paragraph because it mentions the ideas of both paragraphs—industrial pollution and the danger of food modification.

(Answers will vary.)

Possible transitional sentence: Despite the conveniences we enjoy because of modern technology, our lives have not improved in certain ways.

D. Editing the Second Draft (p. 111)

1. Subordinate Clauses

2. Since/Because the jet plane takes us great distances in a short time, we can sometimes see the sun rise more than once in a day. We can sometimes see the sun rise more than once in a day since/because the jet plane takes us great distances in a short time.

3. Because/Since people are stressed, they have trouble relaxing. People have trouble relaxing because/since they are stressed.

2. *Because / Because of*

3. Because of a lack of sleep, people are more likely to catch colds. People are more likely to catch colds because of a lack of sleep.

4. Because they have difficulty sleeping, some people become depressed. Some people become depressed because they have difficulty sleeping.

5. Because they are drowsy, people may have more accidents at work. People may have more accidents at work because they are drowsy.

6. Because of artificial light, people sometimes work at night instead of sleeping. People sometimes work at night instead of sleeping because of artificial light.

7. Because of stress and environmental factors, some people develop short-term insomnia. Some people develop short-term insomnia because of stress and environmental factors.

3. Logical Connectors

2. Modern technology allows us to work 24 hours a day; as a result/consequently, we work more and have less time for sleep.

3. Modern technology has given us more options in our lives; thus/therefore, it is more difficult to make decisions.

4. Fragments

After an overnight stay with the Scouts and their fathers in a big canvas tent, everyone laughed at him at breakfast the next morning. Although they all had great respect for him, his snoring had made him an object of ridicule. Because he couldn't bear the thought of ever being laughed at again, he resigned from his position two weeks later. Despite his ability to help others, Roger had no way of helping himself. Because of this incident, Roger started to lose confidence in himself and turned his back on scouting.

After he explained his problem to a friend, Roger was able to turn his life around. His friend sent him to a doctor that specialized in sleep disorders. By means of a mechanical device, which the doctor prescribed, Roger now has "continuous positive airway pressure" when he sleeps. As a result, he no longer snores.

5. Run-on Sentences and Comma Splices

2. ✓

3. Freud insisted that dreams should be interpreted as unfulfilled and forbidden desires; this theory was not acceptable to Jung.

4. ✓

5. Freud believed that we dream in order to defend ourselves from the stress of daily life. He thought that if we did not dream, everyday life would be intolerable.

6. ✓

UNIT 7
HOW I'LL BECOME AN AMERICAN

II. Reading for Writing

A. General Understanding (p. 122)

1. Identifying Main Topics

Main topics: crime, health, money

Other topics: consumerism, technology, depression, tourism, relationships

2. Discussing Main Ideas

2. Line numbers 19–20: "And I'll buy the best dishwasher, microwave, dryer, and hi-fi in the world—that is, the U.S.A."

3. Line numbers 15–18: "I'll sell my house and buy a condo. I'll sell my condo and buy a mobile home. I'll sell my mobile home and buy an igloo. I'll sell my igloo and buy a tent. As an American, I'll be clever: I'll sell my igloo and buy a tent when I move to Florida from Alaska."

Line numbers 39–41: "I'll try to change my life a little bit. I'll try to exchange my wives, my cars, my lovers, my houses, my children, my jobs, my pets."

4. Line numbers 38–39: I'll be the patient of 12 psychiatrists, and I'll be disappointed with all of them."

5. Line number 33: "I'll work really hard since as an American I wanna be rich."
   Line numbers 53–54: "My second favorite [book] will be How to Be Rich in Seven Weeks. I'll try to follow this advice in seven years."

6. Line number 34: "I'll always be in a hurry: Time is Money."

7. Line numbers 67–68: "As an American, I'll buy a new TV every time a larger screen appears on the market."
   Line numbers 70–71: "Anyway, my living room will look very much like the living rooms you can see in the soaps: nobody will complain."

B. Working with Language (p. 124)

1. Satire: The Language of Humor

1. **Repetition:** Vámos repeats the number "38" for comic effect.
   Unexpected surprise: Vámos surprises us when he says that he has been Hungarian for 38 years, and now he will try to be an American for the next 38.

2. **Putting opposites together:** Vámos puts together the words *fastest* and *slowly*. Pun, *Fastest food* is a pun on *fast food.*
   Unexpected surprise: Vámos says that he'll *retape* a TV show before he tapes it.

3. **Unexpected surprise:** When Vámos mentions foods and drinks, he includes *toothpaste* and *acid rain,* which a person does not eat or drink.

4. **Repetition:** Vámos repeats words that are free of something: *sugar-free, salt-free,* and *lead-free.*
   Unexpected surprise: Vámos says his diet includes *lead-free* gasoline, which is not a food.
   Exaggeration: Vámos mentions that he will get mugged twice and knocked down three times while jogging.
   Unexpected surprise: Vámos says his diet will make him reach 200 pounds. Usually a person on a diet *loses* weight.

III. Prewriting Activities
A. Puns (p. 126)

1. Understanding Puns
The cartoon is a pun because it shows rats racing around Wall Street. "A rat race" means a situation in business or politics where people are always competing against each other. Wall Street, the financial capital of the U.S., is this type of competitive environment, where stocks, bonds, and options are aggressively bought and sold by stockbrokers and others.

2. Identifying Puns

2. "Cut into" is a pun since it means to cut but also to break, or to hurt. The forks and knives can thus mean criticism, sharpness, or failure in communication, which the Taiwanese want to be harmonious.

3. "Laptop of luxury" is a pun because it sounds like the "lap of luxury." (Rich people live in "the lap of luxury.") The writer is saying that the Taiwanese admire high tech people who use and produce "laptop" computers and who have become rich as a result.

4. To "strike a chord" is a pun in this sentence because it is an idiom with two meanings: To make a musical sound by touching the strings or keys of an instrument, and to cause a person to have a particular emotion or memory.

5. "Worth its weight in gold" is a pun because it has two meanings—expensive and to weigh a lot (because gold is costly and heavy). The Taiwanese hide piles of gold in their homes; therefore, even though their houses are cheap-looking and in bad shape, their homes are very valuable.

IV. Structured Writing Focus
A. Starting to Write (p. 128)

1. Before You Brainstorm
Student essay first draft

1. No. There is no reference to American or Japanese cultures in the introduction.

2. No. The thesis statement is not clear because we don't know what the "three secrets" are about.

3. The third body paragraph needs to be developed more with examples of things you should not do in Japan.

4. The conclusion does not remind us of the thesis statement.

Student essay second draft

1. The introduction in the second draft is much more interesting because it describes the differences between the Japanese and Americans.

2. The thesis statement is more comprehensive. It announces the topics of each body paragraph.

3. More examples and details have been added to the third body paragraph to explain what a person should not do. For example, you should never praise a meal you have prepared for guests—you should say what a terrible cook you are.

4. *First of all, For instance, Second, For example, Third*

5. The conclusion of the second draft is much more understandable. It restates the main idea from the introduction: that Japan is a small island where people have to obey the rules of society in order to live in harmony.

D. Editing the Second Draft (p. 134)

1. Causatives

  2. ✓   6. feel

  3. study 7. ✓

  4. ✓   8. feel

  5. consume   9. to disappear

2. *-ing/-ed* Adjective Endings

  2. overwhelmed 5. nurtured

  3. surprising   6. interested

  4. amazed   7. fascinating

UNIT 8
FOR AND AGAINST BILINGUAL EDUCATION

II. Reading for Writing

A. General Understanding (p. 142)

1. ESL programs are taught entirely in English; bilingual programs are taught in the students' native language and English is one of the subjects they learn.

2. They were afraid that their children would never learn English and would fall behind in their academic subjects.

3. They were afraid that their teenagers would fall behind in their academic work and drop out of school because of culture shock.

4. Some parents want their children to be able to communicate with their families, to remember their native language, and to be able to communicate on trips home to their native country.

B. Working with Language (p. 142)

1. adjust to
2. thrived
3. proficient
4. declined
5. expected to
6. refused
7. on an equal footing
8. supportive
9. stood solidly behind, catch up with
10. educated
11. concerned

III. Prewriting Activities

A. Categorizing Arguments For and Against Bilingual Education (p. 144)

1. Identifying Arguments

1. F	2. F	3. A	4. A
5. F	6. F	7. A	8. A
9. F	10. A	11. F	12. A

2. Categorizing Arguments

Cultural Arguments

For Bilingual Education: 1, 6

Against Bilingual Education: 10, 12

Economic Arguments

For Bilingual Education: 2, 11

Against Bilingual Education: 4, 7

Educational Arguments

For Bilingual Education: 5, 9

Against Bilingual Education: 3, 8

IV. Structured Writing Focus

A. Starting to Write (p. 146)

2. Thesis Statements for Argumentative Essays

2. This is not a good thesis statement. It states an opinion, but it does not give arguments that the writer can develop in the body paragraphs to support his/her opinion.

3. This is a good thesis statement because it clearly expresses the point of view that bilingual education does not offer what immigrants need: specialized services, exposure to English, and time to adjust to American customs. In the body

paragraphs the writer will develop these three ideas.

4. This is not a good thesis statement. The writer does not take a stand or show a clear point of view.

5. This is a good thesis statement. The writer will explain his/her point of view—that English should be the only language for people in the United States because of economic, cultural, and educational factors.

6. This is a good thesis statement. The writer clearly shows his/her point of view—that parents, not school administrators, should decide whether bilingual education is appropiate for their children. In the body paragraphs the writer will discuss psychological, cultural, and economic reasons for this argument.

D. Editing the Second Draft (p. 153)

1. Present Unreal Conditionals

1. were made illegal
2. would learn
3. were banned
4. would lose
5. would be

2. Connectors

3. Despite the fact that immigrants respect their native culture, they often come to value cultural aspects of American life.

4. Despite knowing little English at first, some immigrant children can learn it very fast.

5. Despite the fact that it is the main language of the United States, English has never been recognized as the official language.

6. Despite the fact that it limited immigration in the past, the United States welcomes immigrants today.

For bilingual education
(Answers will vary.)

2. Although immigrant children should be encouraged to speak English at school as soon as they can, they should be taught some subjects like math and science in their native language so they don't fall behind in these subjects.

3. Even though immigrant children should not be permanently separated from children who are native speakers, they

should take bilingual education classes at first so they will not feel isolated from their classmates.

Against bilingual education
(Answers will vary.)

2. Even though some people say that children do better with their school subjects when they are taught in their native language, immigrant children need to speak English as soon as possible, so they should study all subjects in English.

3. Despite the fact that immigrant children may feel lonely at first in an all-English classroom, they should be put in all-English classes so that they will not be separated from native speakers at school.

UNIT 9
CASE STUDIES IN BUSINESS ETHICS: MALDEN MILLS AND BEN & JERRY'S ICE CREAM

II. Reading for Writing

A. General Understanding (p. 162)

1. Categorizing Topics about Malden Mills
1. a, e, g   2. b, k   3. i
4. d, f, j   5. c, h, l

2. Making a Controversial Decision
Effects on Workers and Community:

2. The workers had good morale because their jobs were saved, and as a result they remained loyal to the company.

3. The workers were able to financially support their families until the factory was rebuilt.

Effects on Company and Shareholders:

2. By rebuilding in Lawrence, the company did not have to face the "unknowns" of relocation to a foreign country, such as new workers and different international laws regulating their trade if they located the factory outside the United States.

3. Paying the workers during rebuilding lowered stockholder dividends. On the other hand, the shareholders benefited from a quality product (given the employees' specialized knowledge), which insured the long-term value of their stock.

B. Working with Language (p. 163)

1. b   2. b, c   3. a

4. a   5. a   6. c

III. Prewriting Activities

A. General Understanding (p. 166)

1. Categorizing Topics about Ben & Jerry's

1. b, f   2. a, e, h   3. c, f, g

4. d, j, l   5. i, k

IV. Structured Writing Focus

A. Starting to Write (p. 168)

2. Brainstorming

Point of Comparison: The companies' contributions to charities

Similarities: Both help local and international charities. Both help the homeless.

Differences: B&J gives to environmental charities, community clean-ups, literacy, and world peace. MM gives to the Red Cross and donated emergency blankets to Turkey after the 1999 earthquake.

Point of Comparison: The companies' treatment of their workers

Similarities: Both companies pay their workers good wages. Both companies give their workers full benefits packages.

Differences: MM helps its employees buy homes. B&J paid its executives no more than 5 times what it paid its workers.

Point of Comparison: The companies' policies toward the local community

Similarities: Both companies have supported the local community.

Differences: MM has supported Lawrence, Massachusetts, by rebuilding the factory there and saving 3,000 jobs. B&J has supported Vermont by buying milk from local Vermont dairy farmers.

B. Preparing the First Draft (p. 169)

1. Thesis Statements for Comparison and Contrast Essays

Sentence 3 is an effective thesis statement because it clearly compares two subjects—small and large grocery stores—using three points of comparison.

1. Main idea: Small groceries are better.

2. Main idea: Department stores are better.

3. Main idea: Franchise restaurants are better.

2. Organizing Ideas from the Thesis Statement

2. Body paragraph 1: Department stores are less convenient than mail-order catalogues.

Body paragraph 2: Department stores give greater choice.

Body paragraph 3: Department stores allow people to try on clothes before buying them.

3. Body paragraph 1: Owning an independent restaurant allows more creativity and individuality.

Body paragraph 2: Owning a restaurant franchise involves less financial risk.

Body paragraph 3: Owning a restaurant franchise includes management training.

3. Transitional Sentences

Practice Selecting Transitional Sentences

1. b   2. a   3. c

D. Editing the Second Draft (p. 174)

1. Connectors Showing Comparison and Contrast

2. Malden Mills sends Polartec to factories before it comes to stores, while Ben & Jerry's sends its ice cream directly from the factory to food stores.

Unlike Malden Mills, which sends Polartec to factories before it comes to stores, Ben & Jerry's sends its ice cream directly to food stores.

3. Although Polartec and Ben & Jerry's ice cream are different kinds of products, the companies that make them have a lot in common.

Polartec and Ben & Jerry's ice cream are different kinds of products; nevertheless, the companies that make them have a lot in common.

4. Like Polartec, Ben & Jerry's products appeal to the senses.

Polartec appeals to the senses. Similarly, Ben & Jerry's appeals to the senses.

2. Direct Questions and Embedded Questions

(Answers will vary.)

2. Do you know when an employer should consider the needs of the community?

3. Could you explain where an employer of a local factory should do his recruiting?

4. I wonder what employees should expect from their employers?

5. I would like to know what the best proof of an employee's loyalty is.

6. Tell me how employers can get the best work from their employees.

3. Noun Clauses

(Answers will vary.)

2. How much respect a company gives to its employees determines how loyal they will be.

3. Whoever supervises people at the workplace should be fair and kind.

4. What corporations should do for better public relations is to give large donations to charities.

5. How Malden Mills employees responded to the crisis was to help rebuild the factory.

2. what "caring capitalism" is all about

3. What he had always told

4. ✓

5. what he had preached

6. what he believed in

7. ✓

8. ✓

9. ✓

10. How he has done this

UNIT 10
THE TELL-TALE HEART

II. Reading for Writing

A. General Understanding (p. 184)

1. Setting the Stage

1. The narrator wants to kill the old man in order to get rid of his vulture eye.

2. Every night at midnight, the narrator sneaks into the old man's room when the old man is sleeping.

3. The narrator cannot carry out his plan because the old man's eye is always closed.

4. Every morning the narrator is kind to the old man, asking him how he slept, calling him by his first name, never showing how he really feels.

5. The old man wakes up when the narrator makes a noise opening the lantern.

6. The old man is terrified because he hears a sound and feels that he is in danger.

2. Summarizing Events

In "The Tell-Tale Heart" the main character (who is also the narrator) murders the old man because his eye resembles an evil eye and the narrator thinks he must destroy it. Every night for one week the narrator enters the old man's room while he is sleeping, preparing to kill him. But he can never complete the act because he never sees the eye that he hates. During one nightly visit, however, the old man hears a noise and wakes up. The narrator, who is holding a lit lantern, sees the evil eye and is finally able to kill him, by dragging the old man to the floor and pulling his heavy bed over him. The narrator then cuts the body into pieces and hides them under the floorboards. Soon afterward, three policemen arrive at the house to investigate, after neighbors reported hearing a scream. The narrator calmly takes them around the house, explaining that the old man is in the country, and shows them the old man's possessions as proof that nothing out of the ordinary has happened. The narrator then asks the policemen to sit down in the room under which the body is buried.

3. Analyzing the Main Ideas of the Story

2. Line numbers: 37–40, 90–93
   The narrator waits a week until he sees the evil eye open, on the eighth night.

3. Line numbers: 104–108
   The beating of the old man's heart drives the narrator to kill the old man.

4. Line numbers: 125–128
   The narrator frightens the old man with a loud scream. Then the narrator drags the old man to the floor and smothers him with the heavy mattress.

5. Line numbers: 137–148
   The narrator cuts the body apart to hide it. He cuts off the head, arms, and legs, and then places the body parts under the floorboards.

6. Line numbers: 1–8
   The narrator first shows that he may be mad when he tells us that his senses are so acute that he can hear all things in heaven and hell.

7. Line numbers: 19–22, 137–138
   The narrator points out to the reader how calm he is and how well he planned and

carried out the murder, and how cleverly he hid the body. To him, this shows that he cannot be mad. His argument is not convincing, however. The narrator consistently shows that he is mad; for example, he is obsessed with the evil eye. At the end of the story, the narrator also shouts wildly at the police, like a madman.

    8. Line numbers: 153–158

    The policemen come to search the house for a possible crime after a neighbor reports having heard a shriek come from the house.

B. Working with Language (p. 189)

1. sharp, very sensitive
2. clever, crafty
3. fakery, falsehood
4. shocking, terrible
5. looked, stared
6. quietly, secretly
7. careful, watchful

2. cunning
3. dissimulation
4. stealthily
5. wary
6. acute
7. dreadful

III. Prewriting Activities

B. Understanding Plot (p. 191)

Introduction of the Conflict: Lines 1–18

Rising Action: Lines 19–46

Climax: Lines 47–136

Falling Action: Lines 137–168

Resolution of the Conflict: Lines 169–211

C. Evaluating Narrative Point of View (p. 193)

(Answers will vary.)

1. Poe has the main character tell the story of his murder plot for these effects: First, the first-person point of view makes the evil and horror greater, since the murderer recounts every detail of his planning of the crime and describes his own excited state. In addition, the first-person point of view helps the reader to better understand the irrational mind and motive of the murderer.

2. Poe wants the reader to know everything that the murderer is thinking to make the murder more terrifying.

IV. Structured Writing Focus

A. Starting to Write (p. 194)

1. Before You Brainstorm

Effect of setting and pace on mood

2. The noise of the hinges creaking in such a silent setting creates an ominous, dark atmosphere.

3. The loud yell breaks the silence in a shocking way, creating a violent mood.

2. The narrator's description that he moves slower than time itself increases the suspense.

3. The fast movements coming suddenly after very slow movements make the reader feel that the narrator is now out of control.

Foreshadowing

2. **Symbol:** The death watches symbolize the presence of death, which haunts people, since all people die.

    Future Event Foreshadowed: The death watches foreshadow the old man's death.

3. **Symbol:** The old man's heartbeat symbolizes the old man's life and the narrator's guilt for his murder.

    Future Event Foreshadowed: The old man's heartbeat foreshadows the narrator's later confession.

Irony

2. is dissimulating

3. thinks he hears the old man's heart, but it is his own heart that he hears beating

Theme

(Answers will vary.)

B. Preparing the First Draft (p. 198)

1. Supporting Your Interpretation

(Answers will vary.)

Interpretation B is more convincing because it has examples from the text that support the writer's ideas. Also, the reader can see how Poe uses different elements of fiction to create a suspenseful mood.

Response to "The Tell-Tale Heart"

(Lines 114–115)

(Lines 126–128)

(Lines 140–141)

D. Editing the Second Draft (p. 203)

1. Showing Cause and Effect with such ... that / so ... that

4. The narrator plots his murder with such secrecy that the old man doesn't suspect him of the murder plot.

5. The windows are shut so tightly that no light can enter the old man's room.

6. The narrator listens to the old man's groan with such sympathy that the act of murder is even more shocking to the reader.

7. The narrator becomes so angry when he sees the vulture eye wide open that he cannot control himself any more.

8. The narrator believes he appears so relaxed when the police enter the house that he doesn't think they could possibly suspect him.

9. The narrator hears a heart beating so loudly and quickly that he thinks the policemen hear it too.

2. Simple Present and Simple Past Verbs in an Essay on Literature

2. is
3. became
4. was
5. did not have
6. suggest
7. is
8. has
9. hears
10. loses
11. had
12. understand
13. plays
14. wrote